STANDING DOWN 2017

STANDING DOWN 2017

INTERVIEWS WITH
Retiring MPs

ROSA PRINCE

Biteback Publishing

First published in Great Britain in 2017 by
Biteback Publishing Ltd
Westminster Tower
3 Albert Embankment
London SE1 7SP
Copyright © Rosa Prince 2017

ISBN 978-1-78590-284-0

10 9 8 7 6 5 4 3 2 1

A CIP catalogue record for this book is available from the British Library.

Set in Adobe Garamond Pro

Printed and bound in Great Britain by
CPI Group (UK) Ltd, Croydon CR0 4YY

CONTENTS

PREFACE

This book is the second in what I hope will be a long-running series of interviews with MPs as they hover on the cusp of standing down from Parliament. Thanks to the Fixed Term Parliament Act introduced by the coalition government in 2010, the MPs I spoke to for the first volume had five years to contemplate their departure, and I had six leisurely months to interview them. This time around, things were very different. Every one of the thirteen MPs I spoke to had expected, like most of us, to serve for another three years, taking them to 2020. Instead, when Theresa May decided to go to the country early, they had just days to make up their minds if they wanted to bow out ahead of schedule or stay until 2022.

By virtue of their appearance in this book, all the MPs here decided it was time to go. Their reasons for leaving, however, are as varied as their radically different careers and journeys through the House of Commons. I hope you enjoy their stories as much as I did.

The much shorter time scale involved in producing these interviews means that they were conducted far closer to polling day than was customary last time, with one or two taking place after the election. Lacking the benefit of hindsight, many made predictions for the outcome that turned out to be strikingly far from the mark – though in their defence, they were far from alone in anticipating a Conservative landslide.

I am very grateful for those who gave up their time to relive their Commons experiences with me during this busy and inevitably stressful time, and would like to wish them all the best for their future lives. Thanks too as always to my publishers, Biteback, and agents, AM Heath, as well as to my lovely family.

I look forward to bringing you the memories of the next graduating class of MPs in 2022 – or, perhaps, somewhat sooner.

Rosa Prince
London, July 2017

MICHAEL DUGHER

Michael Dugher, 42, was Labour MP for Barnsley East 2010–17.

How did you end up in Parliament?
'It was an ambition I'd had for a long time, but, I think sensibly, I blew hot and cold on it.'

How did you feel on first becoming an MP?
'Thousands of people, most of them I'd never met, had bothered to come out to vote for me and put their trust in me. I knew it wasn't about me, they were voting for the Labour Party, but as well as being very humbled by the personal support I felt a very strong sense of responsibility on me to be an effective Labour Member of Parliament.'

Best of times:
'I led an opposition day debate once in the last parliament on justice for coalfields. I'd really fought to have this debate, and my grandmother was at our house in Barnsley watching it on TV. I mentioned her father, my great-grandfather, who had been a miner at the pit that I grew up by and died at forty-six of a condition that had the NHS existed would have been easy to have identified and treated. To mention his name at the despatch box, it brought into sharp focus where I came from, and why I was in it.'

Worst of times:
'I knew that it would end in tears at some point, but I committed to serving in the shadow Cabinet. I had a different view of the world in so many ways to Jeremy [Corbyn]. I just felt like a collaborator in a state that was only heading in one direction. I thought I would get fired after the local elections in May [2016]. In the end he decided to pre-empt that, with the revenge reshuffle; I got canned in the January.'

Why are you leaving?
'I like to get things done, I like to make a difference, I like to achieve things, and I feel, and it may be with some sadness I say this, that I can do this more effectively outside politics than I can in the Labour Party at the moment.'

What are your thoughts for future MPs?

'Treat the job and the building with due respect, remember that it's a huge privilege to be there, remember who put you there. Take the job seriously, take the responsibility incredibly seriously, but don't take yourself too seriously. Don't forget it's a job of work like anything else. You're there to get things done. You're not there to stand up and sound off.'

Do you have any regrets about leaving the Commons? And what are you going to do next?

'It is tinged with some sadness that I'm standing down now. It was never Plan A that I would come out after seven years, but it was definitely the right decision, I don't doubt that for a single second. I'm lucky that the thing I'm going to is a great new job. It's a big job and something I'm really excited about. I'm going to be chief executive of UK Music, which is the body that represents all of the music industry.'

MICHAEL DUGHER: THE FULL STORY

Michael Dugher grew up in a mining village in South Yorkshire, coming of age in a time and place which left an indelible mark. Although his family 'were not particularly party political', they had a strong identification with their community of Edlington and its history as a pit village.

His parents were young – just eighteen – when they had him, the first of four children. In 1984, as the young Michael was turning ten, the men of his village walked out on strike, joining in the greatest industrial conflict in the modern era in an ultimately unsuccessful battle against the government of Margaret Thatcher.

Although Mr Dugher's father worked for British Rail (his mother trained as a schoolteacher when he was a teenager), his grandfather had been a miner in the pit their house overlooked, as were the fathers of many of his school friends.

He says:

The miners' strike was an incredibly politicising moment because it was an incredibly traumatic event in that village. The colliery was the main colliery for South Yorkshire. It had been sunk by an ancestor of mine at the beginning of the century.

I remember as a child feeling that something terrible was happening, just having a sense that our country's government was not on our side and was doing something very bad to our community.

At the age of fifteen, Mr Dugher joined the Labour Party. It was a natural step when he got to Nottingham University to become involved in student politics. He rose to become the national chair of Labour Students, based at Labour HQ in London. With the 1997 general election approaching, he was working for the party full time. By now clear that he wanted to make politics his career, Mr Dugher 'blew hot and cold' about whether or not he wished eventually to seek election as an MP. He fought the seat of Skipton & Ripon – unsuccessfully – at the 2001 election. A year earlier, he had gone to work for the Amalgamated Electrical and Engineering Union (AEEU), rising to become head of policy. It was his union background that brought him back to the House of Commons, becoming a special adviser, first to John Spellar, the Transport minister, and then Geoff Hoon, initially at the Ministry of Defence, who became his great mentor.

Serving at the heart of the New Labour government, Mr Dugher was still not sure whether he was ready to take the step to become an MP.

At one level you think, 'I'd like to do this for myself rather than writing things for other people to say.' But equally you saw behind the curtains, you saw the other side of the job, you saw the impact that it can have on family life, the media interest and the long hours that people put in.

Nevertheless, ahead of the 2005 general election he threw his hat into the ring for selection in Doncaster North. 'It

was all going very well until some bright spark called Ed
Miliband dropped into town and blew me out of the water
and I finished second. Our friendship began then, so in a
funny kind of way, it worked out for me.'

Unsure whether or not to try again, Mr Dugher decided
to test out life away from politics, becoming a lobbyist
for Electronic Data Systems, before Westminster in the
form of Mr Hoon, then Labour's Chief Whip, lured him
back. 'That was really my chance to think about whether I
wanted to work in industry or was my heart in politics,' he
says. 'Geoff, who was my boss at the time, he said: "You've
either got it or you haven't and I think you've got it." You
could almost say it's like a drug, with all the downsides
associated with any drug.'

A year later, the then Prime Minister, Gordon Brown,
invited Mr Dugher to spin for him at 10 Downing Street.
Mr Brown was famously difficult, the hours were long and
by now Mr Dugher had a wife and young children.

He was finally clear that he did want to become an MP
himself, however, figuring it could hardly be more demanding than his current job. He says:

In Downing Street, nothing could be as bad as that.
Gordon was not always the easiest person to work for, but
I have a lot of sympathy for him doing that job because

it's a ninety-hour week in Downing Street, which basically means you're working the whole time. My wife was like a single mum for all of that period. I've always been lucky that she's been incredibly supportive.

Mr Dugher was not selected until late in the electoral cycle, ending up in the new constituency of Barnsley East, not far from the town he grew up in.

It was tough, because although I was from thirty miles away, I wasn't from Barnsley. I know it sounds ridiculous but sometimes in these parts of the world that is still an issue. It was so close to the election, I had not yet got a house up there, I was viewed as a bit of an outsider. It was all very rushed.

The seat was nominally a safe one for Labour and, nerves aside, Mr Dugher could be confident of victory. On 6 May 2010, he was elected with a majority of 11,000. It was, he says, a 'humbling' experience.

Having been in and around politics for the entire period of Labour's time in office, Mr Dugher was familiar with the House of Commons, but immediately found opposition a frustration.

'I was in the business end of politics. For me it was always about getting things done,' he says.

The House of Commons, because it is a very special building and so historic, and such an enormous privilege, it does rather go to some people's heads. Which is why some of them will be carried out in a box, because they just can't bear not to have those letters after their name, the doorkeepers saying, 'Oh, hello, sir,' and opening the door, and getting brought their tea in the tea room.

I always tried to be very respectful of the place, to realise what a great privilege it was, but not to let it devour [me].

You see different people on all sides of the House who love to sit in there all afternoon, jumping up and down and doing some intervention, some deeply meaningful, supposedly witty remark, and everyone chuckles. That was never me.

Sometimes you feel that you're working in a cross between a museum and a tourist attraction where some of the artefacts seem to have been there a long time and sometimes move about a bit. For me, the only show in town was about being in government.

Although the frustration with opposition would begin almost immediately, at the start of his time in the Commons there was a moment to prize.

When I gave my maiden speech, you talk about your predecessor and the area you represent, and I did feel a real sense of responsibility and privilege. I remember glancing up at the gallery and seeing my mum and dad were there. There are little moments like that you don't forget.

Within a few months, Mr Dugher was appointed a shadow minister on the defence team by his friend Ed Miliband, now Leader of the Opposition. Having been an MP for just eighteen months, he was in the shadow Cabinet. It was a role he felt comfortable in. 'We all have ambition,' he says. 'It would be fibbing to say that you don't. I wanted to serve on the front bench. I wanted to get after the government. I threw myself in and I felt I did a decent enough job. I didn't feel overawed being in the shadow Cabinet.'

He was conscious, however, that he lacked the 'obsessive' streak needed to take the next step up.

Although I think at one point the bookies quoted me 66–1 to be made leader of the party, that was never something that crossed my mind. I have worked very closely with the people who have done that job – it's really tough and demanding. Although I felt I had lots of skills and abilities and things to offer, I never felt that I was good enough to do that job.

There are a lot of my colleagues in Parliament who are absolute political obsessives, who have absolutely nothing else in their lives, and I found that weird. That has never been the case for me.

I worked very hard at the politics, I was very committed to it, I believe in something, I felt I did a good job, but I've got other things in my life. I watch sport, I like going out. I still feel as though being an MP is quite a weird job, and throughout all of that time, I still felt I was a normal bloke.

Although the two were 'chalk and cheese politically and socially', Mr Dugher came to admire the leadership skills of Ed Miliband.

I know he has a lot of critics including on the right of the party, which is where I come from, but I just felt he would have been a good Prime Minister. I felt he had the intellectual power, I felt he believed in something and so I very much wanted him to be Prime Minister.

His heart is with the left, north London, very much an academic, great intellectual beliefs in the primacy of ideas. Although we were socially different, I just always respected him and I always felt that he respected me. We had our moments of profound disagreement but I never lost that respect for him.

Six months before the 2015 general election, Mr Miliband named him shadow Transport Secretary – an appointment which caused much amusement in Mr Dugher's family. 'All the blokes in my family are railwaymen,' he says. 'When

I was shadow Transport Secretary, my dad said: "Isn't it marvellous, only one in our family who knows nowt about the railway and he's shadow Transport Secretary." Which brings you back down to earth.'

As the 2015 election approached, he had high hopes of becoming Transport Secretary.

He held talks with the permanent secretary at the department about his plans and, with the help of a lawyer, drew up detailed legislation.

His gradual realisation on election night that Labour was not going to be able to form a government – and he would not serve in Cabinet – was, he says, 'horrific'.

I had worked really hard in opposition, thrown myself into being an opposition MP and preparing for government. The next day I woke up and I thought, 'I've become an expert on bus regulation. Well, a fat lot of good that will do me now.' That was a really tough day.

For me, politics is definitely not a game. And if it was, it's not the taking part that counts, it's absolutely all about the winning. I just remember a terrible sense of foreboding about a Conservative majority, and I was worried about which direction the party would go, and I just thought: five more years in opposition.

I had a real sense that we were in a very, very precarious position, and that it was a really, really grave defeat.

As disappointed as Mr Dugher was with the outcome of the election, worse was to come. Having backed Andy Burnham in the ensuing contest to replace Mr Miliband, acting as the former's campaign manager, he along with many others was stunned when the far-left Jeremy Corbyn swept to victory in a comprehensive repudiation of the New Labour establishment he had served at the centre of for his entire adult life.

It was an outcome he did not see coming.

I think if you had asked me at the time, I would have said it would have been hard to imagine how we would have got lower than losing an election and the Conservatives forming a majority government. But with all the genius the Labour Party had, like a bunch of coal miners they keep finding new lows.

Being self-critical, I have to acknowledge along with other people on the other campaigns in 2015 that we failed utterly to inspire the membership and particularly the new membership. They just looked at us and felt we all looked and sounded the same.

We failed to convince people that to go down that road with Jeremy would only lead to disaster.

When Mr Burnham agreed to serve in the shadow Cabinet, Mr Dugher felt he ought to follow suit, despite his obvious differences with the new leader, becoming shadow Culture Secretary. 'I asked to be put out of the way in an area that would bring me into the least dispute with Jeremy,' he says. 'Obviously I could never be a shadow Defence Secretary under Jeremy, for instance. It's hard to have an ideological fallout over the arts.'

From the start, Mr Dugher felt out of place with his new colleagues, many of them long-standing left-wingers who had been allies of Mr Corbyn for decades. Mr Dugher was determined not to stay quiet about his differences with the new leadership, taking a contrary view on such issues as immigration and the renewal of the Trident weapons system.

Given Mr Corbyn's own record of voting against the leadership as a backbencher, and his claim to be comfortable with internal debate and even a little 'dissent', Mr Dugher hoped his new role might work out. He lasted four months.

He says:

I felt pretty instantly that in that shadow Cabinet a lot of people were just loving being in the shadow Cabinet: 'Wow, I'm in the shadow Cabinet, I'm speaking at the despatch box, I'm on the front bench, I'm on the telly.' I just thought this was all madness.

The party was going down a terrible, terrible route and

the trajectory was absolutely obvious and so I used the shadow Cabinet, when I spoke in shadow Cabinet and when I did interviews, to argue for the things I believe. I thought, 'We have got to call this out and say look, do you realise where we're heading with all this?'

Maybe if I was a smarter politician I could have shut up about those things and I could have been in the shadow Cabinet for the last two years. But what's the point? If you're not true to yourself, you're not true to what you believe in, and [if] you don't use politics as a chance to say what you really believe and to get things done then you're not making a difference at all, you're just part of the furniture, you may as well be in a museum.

I wasn't sad to go because it was expected, and it was just unsustainable.

Today, Mr Dugher is scathing about the current Labour leadership, watching in despair what he describes as the disastrous media performances of figures such as Diane Abbott. Along with what he views as the incompetence of the current Labour front bench, he sees more sinister forces at work, referencing images of John McDonnell, the shadow Chancellor and Corbyn ally, giving a speech in front of flags representing the Communist Party of Great Britain and Syria's Assad regime. He is particularly concerned about the influence of Seumas Milne, the former

Guardian journalist who serves as Mr Corbyn's chief of staff.

> You look at the front bench and turn on the radio and hear some of our more prominent spokespeople and you think, 'I cannot believe that you are a shadow Secretary of State trying to win an election.' Many of them are clearly not up to it, to use the famous Clement Attlee phrase.
>
> It's not just their competency that's at issue, it's what they believe in. Seumas Milne is a very clever guy, expensively educated, and lives a very comfortable life. I don't doubt his intellect, I doubt his common sense. I genuinely think people like Seumas think that the wrong people won the Cold War. And I don't. I believe communism is the enemy of freedom and was a disaster. I have no solidarity with people holding up flags of the Communist Party of Great Britain, or writing editorials in the *Morning Star* describing [Assad's retaking of] Aleppo as a liberation. I felt very strongly about that and I've no doubt that Seumas does; I just found it amazing that he's in the Labour Party.

Off the front bench, Mr Dugher tried to be constructive, launching a much-praised campaign to oppose cuts to community pharmacies. Such was the gratitude of the pharmacists that a friend joked he would never again have to buy a box of plasters.

But despite gathering the most ever signatures for a healthcare petition, with a million names, he was disheartened when the proposals came before Parliament and the government easily won the vote to implement them.

'It's a small point but an important one, because if you want to do anything about community pharmacies, or anything else, you've got to get into government,' he says. 'Although it was a backbench campaign I got a lot of credit for, in the end it was ultimately a failure.'

By the time Theresa May unexpectedly announced she was going to the country three years ahead of schedule, such was Mr Dugher's disillusion with Parliament that he was ready to call it quits. So low was the mood among many of his right-leaning colleagues in the Parliamentary Labour Party (PLP) that a number were envious of his decision.

> There was this debate about 'Will you serve under Jeremy or not?' 'Are you a collaborator or are you a freedom fighter?' I said to a mate of mine, 'I hope people don't think of me as a deserter.'
>
> I had announced I had a new job, and he said, 'If we are going to use a Second World War analogy, you're like that bloke who escaped from Colditz. Send us a postcard back from Switzerland, you lucky bastard.'

Interviewed before the election, Mr Dugher was clear that

the left of his party would have to take responsibility for what he feared would be a heavy defeat at the polls, and believed Mr Corbyn should stand aside immediately if he was right.

This is the first time in history where the left in the Labour Party, the hard left, the Campaign Group [of socialist MPs], are able to be tested by the electorate. Because up till now, any election that Labour lost, they would blame the right – it's Tony Blair's fault, it's Gordon Brown's fault, it's the right's fault, you weren't left-wing enough.

There's this view that people vote Conservative because the left's not left-wing enough. It's a view that says it's Michael Dugher's tweets, not Jeremy Corbyn being leader of the Labour Party, that lost us the election. Without being too modest about myself, I think that's very unlikely.

For the first time, it's a left-wing manifesto, Jeremy is the leader, Diane Abbott is the shadow Home Secretary, John McDonnell is the shadow Chancellor, the Campaign Group are on the ballot paper at the general election, and we will ultimately find out whether the country is up for it.

I don't think it's going to be a great night for Labour. I don't think the people standing on the stage with the red rosettes are going to be a-cheerin' and a-hollerin'. I may be wrong, I hope I am. I want Labour to win the election.

I've been a Labour Party member for twenty-six years, and it's really important to who I am.

The stakes are very high. It's not about running the Labour Party that's the issue, it's about running the country, because the people who pay the price for a Conservative government are the miners, for instance, the working-class kids that I grew up with, and the people I've represented in Parliament, and that's why I felt so strongly about it.

Although he will miss his constituency, Mr Dugher is relaxed about leaving Parliament. So excited is he about his next job, as chief executive of UK Music, that he is forgoing a vacation and taking up the post even before the election.

The role is a good fit: Mr Dugher credits his love of music with inspiring his later success in life. 'Music has the power to change people's lives; that was certainly the case for me,' he says.

When I went to secondary school, I was fairly average at most things. I was very into music, listening to it, and my grandmother bought me a Spanish guitar and said that if I stuck at it for a year then she would buy me an electric guitar. So I taught myself to play the guitar. It gave me huge amounts of confidence. I would be keen to go to school every day because at lunchtime I could go to the music room and they had a piano. I taught myself piano, and I taught myself bass guitar, and I taught myself drums.

As he faces his new future, Mr Dugher is looking forward to putting his family first.

When you have young kids, it's amazing how quickly they change and grow up, and how fast the time goes, and I just want to hold on to some of that time. I know in truth that my family, who have given me every support for the last ten years, have really played second fiddle to my work in politics. I just feel I owe them a little bit more now.

When you're old and grey and you're in your rocking chair, and you look back at what you've done in life, the job is just a career you've had. You want to have made a difference and what you chose to do may be a big part of that, but you also have got to answer the question: were you a good dad, were you a good husband, were you a decent human being?

While packing up his parliamentary office, Mr Dugher was struck by how much harder it could have been.

I suddenly thought how tough it must be for people, of any party, who through no fault of their own lose their seat because someone on telly who happened to be Prime Minister was deeply unpopular.

You get turfed out and I expect you feel devastated and humiliated and crushed; you've got no plans for the future because you've been throwing yourself at the campaign and you suddenly find yourself, like me, throwing boxes on a trolley. It must be awful.

What will I feel on the day after polling day? I don't care whether they are political opponents or not, I will really feel for those people who lose their seats.

Whatever the public think of us, most of us at least are still human beings.

CV

Raised in Edlington, South Yorkshire, a Labour Party worker and trade union official who went on to work as a special adviser for John Spellar, Transport Secretary, and Geoff Hoon, Defence Secretary and Chief Whip, before serving Gordon Brown at 10 Downing Street.

2001   unsuccessfully fights Skipton & Ripon.
2010   elected MP for Barnsley East, becomes shadow Defence minister and PPS to Ed Miliband, Leader of the Opposition.
2011   becomes shadow minister without Portfolio.

2012   becomes Labour Party vice-chair.
2013   becomes shadow Cabinet Office minister.
2014   becomes shadow Transport Secretary.
2015   becomes shadow Culture Secretary.
2016   sacked from Labour front bench.
2017   stands down from Parliament.

Married to Joanna, three children.

PETER LILLEY

Peter Lilley, 73, was Conservative MP for St Albans 1983–97 and Hitchen & Harpenden 1997–2017.

How did you end up in Parliament?
'I realised that the British system is very open, and if you're not entirely stupid, and indeed sometimes if you are really stupid but you are persistent and determined, it's open to anybody. But it took me quite a long time to get in. I didn't get in until I was nearly forty.'

How did you feel on first becoming an MP?
'I wasn't a natural parliamentary performer, but I loved it. Still do. And I was ambitious.'

Best of times:
'The department I found most rewarding and satisfying was social security, which I did for five years under John Major. I instinctively knew when I got there that I would be there for a full term, because John Major had clearly put me in a department that didn't have anything to do with Europe. And it turned out to be the biggest department in terms of spending by far.'

Worst of times:
'There was a period where I was being subjected to some rather unpleasant personal stuff in the wake of the Back to Basics storm. Fortunately, I have a fairly thick skin and fortunately my wife is a fairly strong character, but my mother and my sister and my brother-in-law found it very unpleasant.'

Why are you leaving?
'I discussed it with my wife before Easter, as I do with each parliament, and she usually wants me to stand down. I had agreed I would stand down at the next general election, assuming it would be 2020. And, low and behold, two weeks later Theresa May announces a general election. And Gail says, "It's the next general election."'

What are your thoughts for future MPs?
'Important: it was even in my day but even more now

– entrench yourself in your constituency in your first term. Get known as a good local Member of Parliament, but ultimately you're there to be a parliamentarian, not a parish politician. And although that's important, you have got to learn the ropes in Parliament. Just sitting in the chamber and asking questions and making speeches is what it's about.'

Do you have any regrets about leaving the Commons? And what are you going to do next?
'I've reconciled myself to it now, so I don't think it will be too painful. I'll certainly remain in the fray politically; I'll write things and speak and argue. Who knows if I'll find myself translated to another place [the House of Lords]. Should I do so, I'll have a platform to do so, but even without that I'll have a platform.

'I'm involved with various business things which give me a way of keeping me out for lunch, which is very important. Although my wife is delighted I'm not standing, she doesn't want to see too much of me.'

PETER LILLEY: THE FULL STORY

Peter Lilley was born in Harpenden in Kent, to a family which took little notice of politics – it was an interest he believes was entirely self-generated, motivated by little more than a contrarian schoolboy's instinct to take an opposing view to those of his peers.

He says of his upbringing:

It was not a political family and they were somewhat bemused that I should have any interest in politics. They thought it was slightly disreputable. My mother was simultaneously proud of my becoming a minister and an MP, but wished I could have done it without having been a politician.

I was always interested in politics, from when I got out of my pram. I started reading a bit, and at school I was in political discussion with my schoolmates. The fashion then was to be left-wing and to think the solution to all our problems was socialism or communism. I was a perverse sort of youth so I just disagreed with them.

By the time he went to Oxford University, Mr Lilley was interested enough to become active in the Conservative Association, but, being 'perilously shy', he steered clear of the Oxford Union, something he now regrets.

After graduating, he became an energy analyst at a stockbroking firm. It was only when he saw that some near contemporaries who had been a couple of years ahead of him at Oxford were starting out on a career in politics that it dawned on him he might do the same. 'I had always assumed you had to have some kind of family connection, which I didn't,' he says.

By now firmly on the right of the Conservative Party, Mr Lilley got involved with the Bow Group, rising to become chairman in 1973. Along the way, however, he incurred the wrath of Ted Heath, the then Prime Minister, who was in the midst of his pet project of negotiating Britain's entry to the European Union (then known as the European Economic Community). To his disappointment, Mr Heath blocked his inclusion on the Conservative candidates' list.

'Although I was insignificant, I had come to the attention of Ted Heath,' Mr Lilley says. 'He thought I was a bad influence because of my views on Europe. Actually I was quite in favour of joining, but I declared myself an admirer of [former French President] General [Charles] de Gaulle, [who had twice vetoed Britain's application to join the Community]. That was a black mark.'

By the time Mr Heath relented and allowed him on to the list, the October 1974 general election was approaching rapidly. Mr Lilley was the last candidate to be selected, winding up in the north London constituency of Tottenham. 'I fought Tottenham and Tottenham fought back,' he says. 'Tottenham was a solid Labour seat but I had a great time and remained attached to it for some years.'

Although he was roundly defeated, Tottenham was important for Mr Lilley on a personal level too. His future wife, Gail, was living locally and serving as secretary of the Keep Britain in Europe movement, which was campaigning to join the EEC in the referendum which would be held in June 1975. She was 'assigned to recruit me', he says. 'I had heard of this very beautiful girl who was at the other end of Haringey. When she rang me up and said would I become involved, I put aside any reservations I had. And duly married her. So I did well out of Europe.'

Although he would later become a leading Eurosceptic, at this stage Mr Lilley did not oppose Britain joining the EEC. 'I had always been in favour of inter-governmental cooperation in Europe, but not a federal Europe,' he says.

> We were officially told that it may look as if it's meant to be a federal project, but the rest of Europe is prepared to abandon that for the delights of having us on board. I was prepared to accept that. Whether it was under the influence of this beautiful girl or not, I don't know.

Mr Lilley now found himself drawn further into national politics, as Geoffrey Howe, who served under Mr Heath in government and opposition, recruited him from the Bow Group to help draw up policy papers and write speeches. Howe introduced him to both Nigel Lawson and Margaret Thatcher, meaning he was intimate with three of the most important people in the party, putting him at an advantage when he finally became an MP.

As the 1979 general election approached, Mr Lilley applied for 'seat after seat', only to be turned down repeatedly. It wasn't until some time after Margaret Thatcher's election, and with another election looming, that he finally landed the plum constituency of St Albans in Hertfordshire. 'By this time I was married, and that seemed to make a difference for some reason,' he says.

> The final round, it was a very close ballot, and I think I won by one vote. In those days they used to ask your spouse a question, and Gail had planned her answer, whatever the question would be, and her answer was that she was a local councillor in Hornsey, been a chairman of her ward, done this, done that. She ended up saying she had stuffed thousands of envelopes. The sort of people who are active party workers, who attended these things, are envelope stuffers and they all cheered. I'm sure that without that *coup de grâce* I would not have picked up that extra vote which got me selected for St Albans.

As the candidate in a safe Conservative seat, Mr Lilley could be confident of entering Parliament at the next election. And when he finally became an MP, after ten years of trying, he immediately felt at home.

I wasn't sure that I would rise to giddy heights [but] I thought the competition in Parliament would be less severe in the sense of the calibre of the people I would be up against than I experienced in business. Actually, I'm not sure that's true. There are some extremely able people in Parliament. It wasn't some group of dumbos that I could expect to cut through like a hot knife through butter.

Thanks to his connections to the Prime Minister and Chancellor, Mr Lilley rose quickly through the ranks, becoming a parliamentary private secretary to Mr Lawson within months. 'Although it took me longer to get into Parliament than most of my cohort, I was better placed than most when I got there,' he says. From there, promotion was rapid. Following the 1987 election he was made Economic Secretary to the Treasury, before being elevated to Financial Secretary. By 1990, he was in the Cabinet, as Secretary of State for Trade and Industry.

The dizzying speed of his ascent was 'fantastic'. It was, however, a difficult time for a Thatcherite – within a few months the Prime Minister was forced out of office. Although he was among those who advised Mrs Thatcher that 'the game was up', and joined John Major's successful campaign team, he was aware from the outset that his by now somewhat more hard-line views on Europe would bring him into conflict with the new Prime Minister.

He was given the thorny task of taking on the spiralling welfare budget, a role he believes Sir John gave him to keep him well away from matters relating to Europe, but which he soon found he had an affinity for.

'It was a tremendous challenge,' he says. 'Everybody said a Conservative in social security should just keep their head down, otherwise if you do anything active you'll be accused of grinding [your foot] in the faces of the poor. I instinctively knew that was wrong, and that we had to do something. It was desirable for society to have less people on welfare and ideally be more generous to them. Most people want to see more people get off welfare and into work.'

Soon after taking up the job, Mr Lilley delivered his now infamous 'little list' speech to the 1992 Conservative Party conference, a parody of Gilbert and Sullivan's 'Behold the Lord High Executioner!' song from the *The Mikado*. He was largely unmoved by the resulting furore – although he does have one regret, a reference to: 'Young ladies who get pregnant just to jump the housing queue...'

'There was one line in it I should have taken more trouble over,' he says.

But I couldn't get anything else to rhyme, is the truth. Even so, it would have got a lot of flak I'm sure. What gave rise to that particular line was the council in St Albans, which was controlled by a Labour–Lib Dem coalition, had actually come to see me to say that something must be done about this problem of having to allocate all our new vacant premises and council housing to single mothers. So I had not thought of it as party politically contentious at all, which was probably poor judgement on my part.

Mr Lilley's move to replace invalidity benefit with a new incapacity benefit, including, for the first time, assessments of whether claimants were capable of work, made him a controversial figure. He became a feature on *Spitting Image*, the satirical television show, where he was portrayed as a Nazi.

'Although I have a reputation of being terribly shy, because I was very shy, I'm quite thick skinned, so it never occurred to me to take it personally,' he says 'I was resolved that if we were to reform social security, we had to win the argument on two levels. We had to win it on the intellectual level … but also you had to win it at a popular level, you had to mobilise public opinion.'

While he took the ribbing over his politics in good spirit, Mr Lilley found persistent untrue rumours through the Major years that he was a closeted homosexual more problematic, mainly because they upset members of his family. He feels he was a victim of the fallout from the Back to Basics scandal, in which a number of senior ministers were caught out in sexual indiscretions, casting suspicion on some of their blameless peers.

While he describes the period as his worst time in politics, he tells a bawdy story about a moment of levity amid the upset.

When Back to Basics was going on and the newspapers were trying to find things out, they came to St Albans and knocked on all the doors, and they went to the pub opposite us, and said to the publican: 'Do you have any dirt on Mr and Mrs Lilley? There is money in it.'

They said: 'you can see his house from here. Do you ever see anything going on?' [The publican] is quite a character, and he said: 'Yes, I can see them, I often see some very strange goings-on. I see him crouching down on all fours, and her leaning over him with a stick.' And they said: 'In the bedroom?' And he said: 'No, no, out in the road. He is looking under the car for bombs, and she is holding the mirror.' Because we had to check under our cars for bombs every day.

Throughout his time in Cabinet, Mr Lilley continued to have a strained relationship with the Prime Minister, a situation which became more fraught as the party tore itself apart over the signing of the Maastricht Treaty, which he opposed. At one point, Mr Major was caught on tape describing three members of his Cabinet, including Mr Lilley, as 'bastards'. Looking back, Mr Lilley believes Mr Major was uncomfortable leading such an undisciplined party. In contrast, Mr Lilley found that he enjoyed the high-wire tension of the late votes and sense that the government could fall at any moment. He reveals he himself came close to bringing the government down over Maastricht. 'It was very exciting,' he says.

I remember after one Cabinet meeting when we had been told by the Chief Whip he couldn't be sure that we would win the vote, it was touch and go, I had to stay behind to talk to John Major about something, and I said: 'Gosh, isn't it exciting.' And he looked at me as if I was quite mad. He was probably correct in the circumstances. He didn't enjoy it. He didn't enjoy being Prime Minister, it was very odd. Even the bits where our future was at stake I found exciting, but it was difficult.

I was torn as to whether I should stay and ensure we got the least bad deal out of Maastricht, or resign. A number of junior ministers came to see me and said: 'Look, if you resign, we'll resign with you.' And that actually made me decide to stay, because if I had resigned, and a number of junior ministers resigned as well, and Cabinet ministers had joined, then the government probably would have fallen. We would have lost our majority. And if we had fallen, there would have been an election, Labour would have taken over and we wouldn't have opted out of the euro, we wouldn't have opted out of the Social Chapter, and so everything that I most feared would have happened. So I decided it would be self-indulgence to leave. And I stayed.

When John Major resigned following the party's trouncing by Tony Blair's New Labour at the 1997 general election, Mr Lilley declared himself a candidate to replace him. He had assumed for some time before the election that he would take part in the leadership race that he had been certain would follow, but when the time came, he began to get jitters about the possibility of victory.

I remember going home to my wife and saying: 'You do realise there is a possibility that I might win. Do we actually want to?' I had worked on the assumption that we would lose that election, and might well win the next one. And actually, after the '97 defeat, it was of such a scale and such a nature, as the weeks went by you realised you had to get into a different mindset. It wasn't the natural thing [that] Conservatives would come back to power for a long time.

And so I sat there with my wife and said: 'Do I want to be Leader of the Opposition and lose the next election, or do I want to be Prime Minister?' And [we] more or less decided that we didn't mind if we didn't win. She was kind enough to say I'd be a better Prime Minister than I would Leader of the Opposition. Which is probably right, I think. I'm better at doing things than opposing things. I certainly wouldn't have been as good as William Hague.

Mr Lilley ended up fourth in the contest, losing to Mr Hague, who he came to admire.

It was an impossible role being Leader of the Opposition between 1997 and 2001, but he did it brilliantly. He was fabulous at Prime Minister's Questions, despite the fact that nobody was taking the Tories seriously. If he had been the Archangel Gabriel and Dante simultaneously we wouldn't have done any better at the next election, but we could have done worse.

Mr Lilley served as shadow Chancellor under Mr Hague, a post he enjoyed but ultimately found frustrating. 'It was a new experience for me,' he says.

It was interesting, but you go from a department with 100,000 people and literally hundreds of people to brief you, to being shadow Chancellor and having one-and-a-half people. It was quite a culture shock. I had to get the party thinking about renewal of policy. And that was a challenge in every sense of the word.

Given his reputation as a right-winger, there is irony that it was a lecture he gave urging the party to accept there should be 'limits to the market', which prompted his departure from the shadow Cabinet, amid suggestions he was repudiating Thatcherism.

William Hague said: 'If one of us has to go it's going to be you, not me.' Seemed fair enough to me. And so I decided I wanted to come off the front bench within a year. It was interesting; a lot of people apparently find it emotionally very difficult, having been a powerful minister, when they become a backbencher. For me it was merely the next step.

The odd thing was, I suddenly realised I had never been a proper backbencher. For most of my first parliament I'd been the Chancellor's PPS ... so I'd never done much backbenching, and when I started doing it and made speeches and so on I kept on getting things wrong, and had to be pulled up by the Speaker: 'A Member of your seniority should know you can't raise a point of order of this sort at this stage,' or 'You can't speak on the main motion when we are at the amendment stage…' So it was rather a late learning curve on how to be a backbencher having mastered being a frontbencher first.

On the back benches Mr Lilley proved an independent spirit, advocating on subjects which went against the political orthodoxy, including the legalisation of cannabis and scepticism over climate change. He says:

> It seemed to me that I ought to raise issues that other people were reluctant to do. I could do so because I clearly wasn't conspiring to get back on the front bench, so I didn't have to worry too much.
>
> There were a whole range of issues that for one reason or another people were just reluctant to consider but which had cropped up in my previous experience. I had come across the drugs issue when I was responsible for customs and excise and found out how much effort we devoted to tackling drugs. It seemed to me that people weren't thinking rationally.
>
> Global warming, similarly, it seemed that Parliament was just not reflecting the full range of argument. So it was up to Lilley to try to redress that. I've been very fortunate in my career in that all the very unpopular and unrespectable views that I have held have subsequently become mainstream.

His final months in Parliament gave Mr Lilley the opportunity to return to the subject closest to his heart – Britain's relationship with Europe.

During David Cameron's attempt prior to the 2016

referendum to renegotiate Britain's role within the EU, Mr Lilley was hopeful that other European nations would prove flexible. He was to be disappointed. 'I had never been a "better off out" person,' he says.

I had hoped that we, over a period of time, could transmit our relationship into one that was much more satisfactory with the rest of Europe, so that it would be like Canada within the North American Free Trade Area rather than like Texas in the United States. I had originally hoped that we could progressively get back powers from Europe that we had, in my view unnecessarily, transferred to Europe.

But when the Prime Minister came back from his negotiation without a single smidgen of a power returned and summoned me in, I said: 'Well, you know my views. You haven't got any back. If it's impossible, then we've got to leave.'

He certainly failed in getting powers back. Whether he tried, I don't know. Whether even if he had gone in with the nuclear threat of leaving, which he clearly didn't really deploy, he would have got any, I doubt it.

The doctrine that power can only move in one direction is so deeply entrenched that probably it would have been impossible for him. I thought it might be [possible], but looking back on how the negotiations worked I think it was a vain hope on my part, and he more or less knew it was a vain hope, and that's why he didn't try very hard. Maybe

he [thought he] would get some sort of cosmetic conces-
sion which would do the trick. And it didn't.

Mr Lilley entered the referendum without much hope of
winning, but looking forward to the opportunity to make
his case for leaving the EU. 'I had seen studies of referenda
and normally they swing to the status quo. So although I
put myself body and soul into it, campaigning and debat-
ing two or three times a day, I assumed we would lose. I
was absolutely convinced.'

As late as the night of the referendum, Mr Lilley was
still sure that his side had lost. 'I went to bed early,' he says.

I heard the Sunderland result and thought: 'that's odd, it
sounds hopeful but don't kid yourself, Lilley.' So I went to
sleep and woke up at 3 a.m. and found we had won. Then
I had a dilemma of whether or not to wake my wife up,
because then neither she nor I would get back to sleep, but I
did wake her up and we both rejoiced. It was extraordinary.

I was always convinced that ultimately it was not possible for the United Kingdom to be part of the United States
of Europe, and that Europe was headed in that direction,
so that either in the gradual way I had formulated or in
the more abrupt way it occurred we would have to change
our relationship.

But I thought it would take longer. I thought we would

lose this referendum, there would be another ten years, and then perhaps we would win later.

Energised by the referendum result, Mr Lilley had not anticipated leaving the Commons within a year of it. But his wife had long urged him to retire, and when they discussed it in Easter 2017, he finally agreed to stand down 'at the next general election' which, like most, he assumed gave him another three years. However, Mrs Lilley was not persuaded that Theresa May's decision to bring the election forward to June 2017 meant that he should serve another full term. He says:

I was tempted to stand again. It was quite a wrench. Making the decision was a bit like going through a bereavement. Anyway, I'm standing down. I thought I'd better get it over and done with. My wife says: 'You're still young enough to do other things.' I hope she's right. I'm not quite sure one can start doing other things at the age of seventy-something. I shall certainly remain in the fray politically, but no longer with a seat in the House of Commons to do it, or a vote in the House of Commons.

There is a flipside. There are aspects of being a Member of Parliament which are quite enjoyable but which are so time-consuming. Above all, constituency correspondence. Much as I love my constituents, they were far too literate.

I have one of the most literate constituencies in the country, and they all spent their weekends writing to me. It was the invention of email which was the final straw.

I've been very fortunate in that every job I've done I've found enjoyable. Maybe I'll find the next phase enjoyable too.

CV

Born in Hayes, Kent, an energy analyst for a stockbroking firm.

1973   becomes chairman of Bow Group.

1974   unsuccessfully contests Tottenham.

1983   becomes MP for St Albans, becomes PPS to Chancellor Nigel Lawson.

1987   becomes Economic Secretary to the Treasury.

1989   becomes Financial Secretary to the Treasury.

1990   becomes Trade Secretary.

1992   becomes Social Security Secretary.

1997   becomes MP for Hitchen & Harpenden, becomes shadow Chancellor and deputy leader of the Conservative Party.

1999   returns to back benches.

2017   stands down from Parliament.

Married to Gail.

GISELA STUART

Gisela Stuart, 55, was Labour MP for Birmingham Edgbaston 1997–2017.

How did you end up in Parliament?

'The only way you can explain it is fate. It was just an accident. I ended up representing the constituency which in 1938 was represented by Neville Chamberlain [despite being German]. But it was also the one with the longest unbroken record of women MPs.'

How did you feel on first becoming an MP?

'There was such a mood of optimism [following the 1997 Labour landslide]. Our whips thought something was wrong if we won a vote with a majority of less than 100.'

Best of times:

'My high point was 23 June last year, I'm afraid [the European referendum]; winning my seat in the 2010 [general] election which everybody thought I would lose and then the referendum which nobody thought we would win. What both things taught me, for better or for worse, is we don't know how history is going to play out.'

Worst of times:

'For me the real low point was falling out with my own party over Europe.'

Why are you leaving?

'There just comes a point when you say, "I just don't want to do this anymore". I think there is one other thing in my life I can do. I don't know what it is, but this is the time to do it.'

What are your thoughts for future MPs?

'My advice is go into politics because at your core you believe there is something that needs to be different. It doesn't have to be a grand view, it may just be one thing that's driving you, but there's got to be a core when you close your eyes and say "this is what I stand for". And if you don't, you just lose your way.'

Will you have any regrets on leaving the Commons? And what are you going to do next?

'It will be the first election for twenty years that I can actually watch the results coming in. I'm really glad the Labour Party and the Tories have selected a woman in Edgbaston so either which way, a woman will continue to represent Edgbaston.

'The advice colleagues give me, and it sounds like terribly sound advice, says that for the next three months you should by and large say "no" to everything.'

GISELA STUART: THE FULL STORY

Gisela Stuart was born in Velden, West Germany, in 1955. She was working as an apprentice bookkeeper when she took a decision which would change her life for ever – she would move overseas to perfect her English. Feeling that the best way to achieve her aim would be to work in a university bookshop, she applied for jobs in countries including including South Africa, Canada and Australia. Manchester Polytechnic made her an offer, and she arrived in this country at the age of just nineteen. She has been here ever since. 'When I went for selection in Birmingham, they said, "Never mind being born in Germany; it's the ten years you spent in Manchester we won't talk about,"' she says.

Although Mrs Stuart had always taken an interest in current affairs, she took a long time to become active in politics. 'I'm probably the most unlikely politician you can think of,' she says.

I didn't join a political party until I was in my mid-thirties. I had taken a career break when my kids were small, and I wanted to kick-start my brain, so I took a law degree, and then I started a PhD at Birmingham University. I had been interested in politics but I never thought, given the first-past-the-post system, that the British would vote for a German.

Her studies led her to develop an interest in pension provision for women. She says:

Something occurred to me, which was that the reason women could not build up proper pensions was because the entire system of pension saving was based on taxable income. If you had low wages or had a career break or were a carer, you could actually not make provision for your old age. That got me to the point where I realised the only way to change things was to become a legislator. That was the link into politics.

Ambitious to become a Labour MP, Mrs Stuart volunteered, as a first step, to fight the 1994 European elections, and unexpectedly came within a whisker of winning. 'I lost by half a per cent and that gave me credibility as a candidate,' she says.

With the 1997 general election approaching, and Labour having adopted all-women shortlists, Mrs Stuart decided to seek selection in the constituency of Stourbridge, where she had developed close relationships with local activists during her run for the European Parliament. Shortly before the Stourbridge selection, however, she threw her hat into the ring in nearby Edgbaston, primarily as a trial run. To her surprise, she won. She says:

I can write you the guidebook on how not to get selected. I didn't realise until after the election that I had actually picked Neville Chamberlain's old constituency. Had I known that I probably would have looked somewhere else, because I would have thought that was really audacious.

I got to the selection meeting and there were five candidates and I literally did not know one person in the room. I wasn't trying to get elected; this was not the meeting I wanted to get adopted in. Essentially I gave a truncated version of the speech Tony Blair gave to the special Clause IV conference [held in 1995, which ended Labour's commitment to nationalisation] and I got the nomination.

With hindsight, Edgbaston and I were a match made in heaven, only we hadn't realised it before. I was comfortable in the seat and they were comfortable with me.

At the time of Mrs Stuart's selection, Edgbaston was held by the Conservatives with a majority of more than 4,000. The seat was one of the first to declare on election night, 1 May 1997, and the scale of Mrs Stuart's victory, which saw Labour's vote share increase by 10 per cent, was an early indicator of the landslide to come. Mrs Stuart's delighted face became an emblem of the night, turning her into an overnight celebrity.

She says:

It's the pub quiz question – I was not the first Labour gain of the night; the first Labour gain as was Claire Curtis-Thomas [in Crosby], but because no one expected Claire to win there were no TV cameras there, so I was the first televised Labour gain of the night. So I gained a prominence that was entirely gratuitous.

Mrs Stuart remains proud of her role in the early Blair government, a period she feels is under-appreciated by today's Jeremy Corbyn-led Labour Party.

She says:

I look back on that first term of a Labour government and we did do some big things that I regret are not sufficiently appreciated, such as introducing the minimum wage.

It's just sad that it's going to take us a bit of time in

the Labour Party to realise that rubbishing Blair and that Labour landslide is very foolish.

Mrs Stuart became a junior minister at the Department of Health in 1999, working under Alan Milburn, the then Health Secretary.

It was in this role that she experienced one of her worst days in politics when, during the 2001 general election campaign, she accompanied Tony Blair on a hospital visit in Birmingham, giving her a ringside view when he was confronted, live on television, by an angry woman called Sharon Storer, complaining about the care given to her partner, a cancer patient. It was one of a series of catastrophes which hit the party's politicians that day, soon dubbed 'Wobbly Wednesday', but did little to dent New Labour's popularity. Mrs Stuart says:

It started off with Jack Straw being slow clapped at the Police Federation, then there was Tony Blair, and it ended with [Deputy Prime Minister John] Prescott punching someone. I stood in the middle between Storer and Blair, and it was so noisy that I couldn't hear what was going on so I just smiled, because, if in doubt, smile. I've had better days than that.

Following the 2001 general election, Mrs Stuart's next role

would have far-reaching consequences for herself and, ultimately, the country. Mr Blair appointed her a parliamentary representative to the European Convention, tasked with drawing up a new European Constitution.

Mrs Stuart emerged from the negotiations a Eurosceptic, having broadly been in favour of the European project until then. Subscribers to the butterfly effect – which holds that tiny acts can result in fateful and potentially global consequences – will be tickled by the notion that Mr Blair's misguided assumptions about his German MP's attitude towards the EU may have led directly to British withdrawal two decades later. As a direct result of her time in Brussels negotiating the failed constitution, Mrs Stuart became a key leader of the Leave campaign, encouraging many Labour voters to back quitting the Union.

She says:

I do admit I carry a burden of responsibility for some of these things. Negotiating the European Constitution, that was significant for me, because it changed my mind. Having grown up in a federal state, I actually never had a problem with a federal structure. I know it can work. But it requires democratic checks and balances.

I thought we got to the point where we had a model I thought could work. And then it was the last twenty-four hours when the nation state negotiators barged in and removed what I thought were democratic checks and balances. That was the moment when I thought: 'no, this isn't going to work.'

The Convention was run by a thirteen-member presidium headed by Valéry Giscard d'Estaing, the former French president. It also included Michel Barnier, representing the European Commission; as Europe's chief negotiator for Brexit, Mr Barnier is currently Theresa May's bête noire.

Mrs Stuart, who represented the national parliaments, found Mr Barnier a complex character: 'I think Barnier struggled with the role he had to fulfil as Commissioner,' she says. 'He is a Frenchman to the core. I actually find him likeable, but he is not someone who I would regard as nimble or flexible in the negotiation.'

Mrs Stuart has some advice for Mrs May and David Davis as they enter into negotiations with Mr Barnier over Brexit:

He should not be underestimated. He will be a serious negotiator; I don't think he's a negotiator who plays games.

I will watch with interest how they deal with stuff like defence and intelligence sharing; national security. The Commission-man Barnier will understand that the British bring an awful lot to the table, and that both sides seriously diminish themselves if they make anything difficult in terms of working together. Barnier, as a Frenchman, who since [former President Charles] de Gaulle have had an unease about NATO and European defence, will have different instincts. I don't know which instincts will win.

In another example of the butterfly effect, Mrs Stuart also claims to have been responsible, inadvertently, for the creation of Article 50, the section of European law introduced under the 2009 Lisbon Treaty, which sets out a two-year process for departure, and which Britain is currently utilising to quit the EU.

She says:

I remember at the very beginning [of the European Constitution negotiations], meeting ministers at the Foreign Office. I said: 'Look, whatever the outcome of this, I think there are three things we need to get this through Parliament. The three things I wanted were: removal of the words 'ever closer union', an exit clause – a clause to leave – and a clause to allow powers to go to Brussels and be returned from Brussels. A two-way valve.

The Foreign Office was cross with me about wanting the exit clause, because they said that's not a priority for us. But I kept pushing for it. But then what I got, which they thought was terribly clever, was an expulsion clause.

The original clause in the European Constitution says that any country that fails to ratify the constitution within two years will be asked to leave. And they thought that this would shut the British up. Because the one country they assumed would have a problem with the ratification was the UK.

In the end, the constitution died after being rejected in referendums held in France and Holland. But the draft constitution, including the 'exit clause' included to appease Mrs Stuart, went on to form the basis of the subsequent Lisbon Treaty.

She says:

The Lisbon Treaty comes, and, in finest EU tradition, you can never remove anything, and so the expulsion clause becomes Article 50. So you've still got two years, and it is totally arbitrary. Why two years? That's why Article 50 is so ill-thought out because it was never meant to be a clause which would facilitate leaving.

Following her experiences in 2003, Mrs Stuart warned today's Brexit negotiators not to be surprised if the process becomes complicated at the eleventh hour. 'I've been through all this,' she says.

Because the parameters are that nothing is agreed until everything is agreed, the big things will happen in the final hours. The things that turned me to sceptic were the things that happened in the last seventy-two hours.

When it comes to a marathon of negotiation, we tend to be stronger. British negotiators go in having cleared everything across their own government. They've squared Whitehall. Whoever is there will know they have the entire machinery of government behind them, which is not really the case with others. But when it comes to playing poker, when it comes to the final stretches, this is something the Brits are not used to and I think that's something they need to be aware of.

At times during the European Constitution negotiating process, Mrs Stuart relieved her frustration by amusing herself at the expense of her fellow negotiators. As she cleared out her House of Commons office recently, she unearthed a note passed to her by a British official, reading: 'Winding up the French in general and Barnier in particular may be fun but I urge you to stop it now. Because it's getting dangerous.'

On another occasion, as the group went through EU treaties line by line to discuss whether to move from unanimity to qualified majority voting, a 'bored' Mrs Stuart decided to make mischief with a clause relating to the 'merry-go-round' which sees the European Parliament move from Brussels to Strasbourg.

We had literally to go through clause by clause. And of course it was a bit boring for me, because I would have to say: 'Just for the sake of completeness, I object.' And because I was the only one objecting, got absolutely nowhere. I got to the point where I really started to lose it, so I said: 'There is one article which currently [is an issue on which there is] unanimity [voting] where the British government are very keen to move to qualified majority, and this was the one.' And they all kind of looked around and I could see them thinking: 'The British have finally seen the light.' Until they realised what it was. And Giscard just looked at me and said: 'Very amusing, Mrs Stuart, very amusing.'

On her return to the UK, and in a forerunner of the debates which would take place a decade later, Mrs Stuart argued strongly that the proposed Constitution should be put to a referendum. In Tony Blair's pro-European Labour Party, that put her at odds with many of her colleagues.

The worst day of my life in parliament was just before the 2005 election in Committee Room 14 [where the Parliamentary Labour Party meets]. There were four of us who had been campaigning for a referendum: Graham Stringer, Frank Field, Kate Hoey and me. The room was packed full of people and we were personally and individually denounced by colleague after colleague. And we answered back and said, 'you're making a mistake'. I could see Madame Guillotine sitting at the back of the room, knitting. That was really horrible.

Chief among Mrs Stuart's tormentors was Geoff Hoon, then the Chief Whip. She could not help a moment's schadenfreude when he was later caught up in a lobbying scandal and barred from Parliament for five years. She says: 'The thing that in hindsight was quite funny was that Geoff Hoon, who was the Chief Whip, screamed at me for ten minutes, and then of course he was the one who was banned from entering Parliament. And I thought, "you know, it's amazing how quickly things change".'

The process of negotiating at the heart of Europe left an indelible impression on Mrs Stuart, inspiring a Euroscepticism which only solidified as the years passed. 'It was an extraordinary experience,' she says.

I tried to give up the subject of Europe, unsuccessfully. From 2005 onwards, the whips kind of knew that if it had got the word 'Europe' on it, Gisela goes kind of funny. I never changed in my views and the EU [never] changed. This is the thing which made me vote Leave: if this institution, the EU, which everyone says requires change, is incapable of and unwilling to change, even when you're threatened with the second largest contributor, which is Britain, leaving, when is it going to change?

As she approached the 2010 election, with Labour in decline under Gordon Brown, Mrs Stuart knew she had a fight on her hands to remain in Parliament. Always a swing seat, Edgbaston became a target for the Tories. '[It] was the most horrendous election campaign I ever fought,' she says. 'In personal terms it was it exhausting. Everyone thought I would lose, including me. So, 2015, I said, "this is the last election I'm fighting".'

Following the coalition government's introduction of fixed term parliaments, Mrs Stuart assumed she would serve until 2020 – 'By which time I would have done twenty-three years as an MP, who was meant to be just a one-term MP,' she says.

Instead, events turned out otherwise, and Mrs Stuart's final term turned out to be far shorter, more interesting and a great deal more eventful than she could have imagined.

First she began serving on the Commons' Intelligence and Security Committee, which oversees the work of MI5, MI6 and GCHQ, describing it as 'genuinely a privilege'.

'That committee [is] serious grown-ups dealing with se-rious grown-up subjects, nobody grandstanding, there are no press releases in this. You do it in secure rooms having signed the Official Secrets Act, and yet you know you are doing something important. That felt good.'

Then, last June, came the referendum on Britain's member-ship of the European Union, something she had effectively been arguing about for more than a decade. Mrs Stuart became one of the leading campaigners for leaving the European Union, giving the movement much-needed cross-party support, and helping moderate its image as a vehicle for the right.

Like most people, Mrs Stuart began the campaign assuming that Leave could not win. It was only after the referendum was over, with her side emerging victorious, that she was truly able to appreciate the scale of what she had achieved.

> With the referendum campaign there were essentially five of us running a general election campaign. What is so curious is that when you are fighting a campaign like the referendum campaign, where I did the big stuff, I did the TV debates, you don't watch the media yourself. All I saw was I was getting a bus to Wembley Stadium, and we were there for a couple of hours and then you get the bus back home, and then you're tired when you get up the next morning. You yourself have no sense of what is reported out there.

'Sometimes it was very uncomfortable,' she goes on.

> I still think it was the right thing to have done, but having campaigned on the basis of not planning to have won, I was simply trying to run the best campaign on something I felt was right. All you can do is take a deep breath and say, 'do I think this is right?' And then it succeeded.

Despite the exhilaration of victory, Mrs Stuart was not tempted to change her mind about standing down when Theresa May unexpectedly brought the election forward by three years. 'You've just got to know when it's time to go,' she says.

> To win a seat like Edgbaston, to fight in a marginal seat, people just don't realise [how hard it is]. I now regard it as a major luxury that I can have Saturdays off. I've spent twenty-three years thinking a weekend was one day off. So that's why I am leaving. I just felt it was time to go.

Mrs Stuart says goodbye to the Commons with some concerns about those who will succeed her. She laments what she sees as the narrow world view of the Corbynistas, who she feels fail to appreciate the primary importance of electability.

> This is where I think there is a problem with the Labour Party at the moment, and I have put it brutally to some of the Momentum people [the grassroots organisation that supports Jeremy Corbyn]. If you only want to be a movement, if it's a single issue, then you can go join Amnesty International. If it's about a faith you have in something out there, go join your local church.
>
> But if you want to be someone who believes in something, and wants to take the responsibility to bring about change,

and with that make some hard decisions because there are trade-offs here, that's when you join political parties.

If we want to be a party of government, then that requires a willingness to take responsibility. And not just be a list of grievances and a list of issues. That's not what a political party is. There is more to it.

While she is not yet ready to retire, Mrs Stuart is not entirely sure what she will do next, and is aware that she will need to take some time to adjust to life outside the Commons. She says:

You come out, and you spent twenty years being more than you. It wasn't 'Gisela Stuart,' it was 'Gisela Stuart, the MP for Birmingham Edgbaston'. And I think that's the biggest bit to deal with, that you're no longer somebody. That's beginning to sink in and I think that's the bit you just have to come to terms with.

She will spend the next few months working on a chapter of a new book about women MPs, before looking around for something substantial to take on.

It's easy to panic by saying 'Oh my God, my diary is empty, what am I going to do?'

The trick is to find something, not just to keep yourself

busy, the trick is to find something which is a proper job, which is the right thing for you.

We'll see. I'm a great fatalist, you know. The right things happen.

CV

Born Gisela Gschaider in Velden, Bavaria. Begins an apprenticeship in bookkeeping before moving to UK. Trains as a lawyer and begins a PhD in trust law.

1994   unsuccessfully contests European constituency of Worcester & South Warwickshire.
1997   elected MP for Birmingham Edgbaston.
1999   becomes Health minister.
2001   becomes UK parliamentary representative to the European Convention.
2001   serves on Foreign Affairs Committee.
2010   serves on Defence Committee.
2015   serves on Intelligence and Security Committee.
2016   chair of Vote Leave ahead of the EU referendum.
2017   Stands down from Parliament.

Widowed in 2012 on death of second husband, Derek Scott. Two sons.

SIR SIMON BURNS

Sir Simon Burns, 64, was Conservative MP for Chelmsford 1987–97, West Chelmsford 1997–2010, and Chelmsford 2010–17.

How did you end up in Parliament?
'It was the twenty-four hours after [President John F. Kennedy] was shot that I suddenly thought that public service would be a wonderful career and that's what I wanted to do. So I then geared everything in my life to trying to realise that dream as soon as possible.'

How did you feel on first becoming an MP?
'It wasn't as daunting or as difficult [for me] as it was for new MPs, including those today, because I at least knew

how the system worked, where the different buildings and offices were, and everything else.'

Best of times:

'In the House of Commons, the high point was David Cameron appointing me Minister for Health in May 2010. In Chelmsford, it was saving 250 jobs in March '92 for a defence contract where the redundancy notices were all prepared. They were going for a contract to supply upgraded night equipment for the army. An American company was tendering for it as well. It looked like the American company was going to get it. I managed to persuade Alan Clark, who was a Defence Procurement minister at the time, to give the job ... to the company in my constituency, which meant that 250 jobs were saved.'

Worst of times:

'It was a nightmare from '97 until the arrival of [David] Cameron. It was quite obvious that at no time during that period were we going to win the next election. There was nothing you could do. Particularly the period '97 to 2001, and rightly so given the circumstances, the only thing the press and everyone else was interested in was watching what the first Blair government was doing. And we were, to all intents and purposes, irrelevant.'

Why are you leaving?
'I announced fairly early that I wouldn't be standing at the next election, assuming it was 2020. I would be sixty-seven years old, I would have been there 34-odd years – it would then be time to go. When the bombshell came in April that there was going to be an early election, I had to think very quickly. I decided, let's go when people are saying "Won't you stay?" rather than go when people are saying, "God, when is the old bore going?"'

What are your thoughts for future MPs?
'Be true to yourself, always tell the truth to your constituents as to what you are going to do and then do it. Don't try to be too clever by half because you will always get caught out. And, most importantly, never forget who sent you to this fantastic job. It is your constituents, and if you take them for granted, if you don't work as a hard-working constituency MP, then it will be a very difficult life for you. Work hard as a constituency MP, be part of the local community, and you can't go too far wrong.'

Do you have any regrets about leaving the Commons? And what are you going to do next?
'Genuinely none. What I really want to do is be a visiting lecturer at an American university. I have got a trial run at a university down in Georgia in September, which, if

that could come off, would be wonderful, because I adore America and I am very interested in American politics.'

SIR SIMON BURNS: THE FULL STORY

Sir Simon Burns was born in Nottingham but moved with his family to Ghana when he was a small child. His political awakening did not come until he returned to the United Kingdom as a schoolboy, when he began an abiding love affair with the United States and American politics, particularly – unusually for a Conservative – the great Democratic President John F. Kennedy.

Sir Simon says:

My father was not very keen on politicians at all, and until I became an MP I don't think he was thrilled by my interest in politics either. The reason that I became interested and wanted to become a politician actually [took place] when I was nine; it was the evening and the day of 22 November 1963, when John Kennedy was assassinated.

I was brought up in Ghana where we had no television and I had never seen a newspaper, and I was sent back to England in September 1960 to go to boarding school. A bit later, I started to watch television [because] we were allowed to watch the television news and we had newspapers, and I suddenly came across this amazing American President who was forty-three or forty-four. Our Prime Minister was, I think, sixty-nine, the President of France was seventy-nine, the Chancellor of Germany was in his eighties. I suddenly thought, here is a cool individual with an attractive wife and a young family, and I became interested in politics from that point.

In his desire to become an MP, Sir Simon saw no contradiction between supporting the Conservatives and his he President Kennedy's background as a Democrat. 'Both my parents were staunch Tories, regardless of what my father thought of politicians, and I just became a Tory because of my background, my family influence; I never questioned it,' he says.

When I was a student or in my teens, I never had a moment of doubt. I have always been a Tory. Oddly enough, so have my children. No rebels at all. It's simplistic to say Labour – Democrats, and Republicans – Tory. The way that the Republican Party has changed the last twenty years, it's not the Tory Party. It may be certain extreme wings of the Tory Party but it isn't [the mainstream Conservative Party]. The reason I am a Democrat is because of John Kennedy in particular, Bobby Kennedy, but also because of their commitment to healthcare. I passionately believe in the National Health Service. The British people, including myself, are more than happy to pay our tax pounds to have free healthcare without ever having to worry that if you or a family member have a cataclysmic health episode you are going to be bankrupt or you're not going to get the care because you cannot afford it. And the Democrats are like that. They believe in universal healthcare, albeit in a slightly different format to us. To me, health is the most important thing.

Back in 1963, the schoolboy Sir Simon set about doing whatever he could to realise his dream of going into politics. He says:

What I wanted to be was an MP, so I did things that may or may not have helped. I took as many O-levels as I could so that it would look good on a CV. I worked hard. I was determined to get to Oxford if I could, which I did.

During his time at university, Sir Simon immersed himself in Conservative politics, and, on graduating, found himself much in demand. He says:

When I was leaving Oxford, I had three job offers. I was offered a job at the Conservative Research Department, I was offered a job to run Ted Heath's office, and I was offered a job as an assistant to Sally Oppenheim, and I clinically sat down and thought the best job would be working for Sally Oppenheim.

Sally Oppenheim was the MP for Gloucester at the time, a high-profile character who would later serve as a minister. Sir Simon says:

This was in June 1975, and Sally Oppenheim was in Margaret Thatcher's shadow Cabinet. I thought, given the relationship between Heath and Thatcher, it wouldn't be a clever move to take that job, and the job with Oppenheim, apart from the potential opportunities, seemed more interesting, more fun to me than going to work for the Conservative Research Department. So I did that, and it was probably the best decision I took.

Sally Oppenheim was extremely helpful and supportive of me becoming a Conservative MP. I worked for her for six years. This was at a time when not that many Conservative MPs had assistants because the taxpayer didn't pay the salaries for assistants, only paid for secretaries to do the secretarial work.

I then in July 1980 went for the candidates' selection board where they told me I had passed but they would not put me on the approved list of candidates until I had got another job, because the only job I had done was working for Sally Oppenheim in the House of Commons. I was fortunate in that she persuaded her son, Philip, to make me a director of his small publishing company. I then moved from her to her son. He had a what turned out to be very successful business which he had started up from scratch publishing the business equivalent of *Which?* magazine for consumers. So I had got another job with different experience and so they put me on the candidates list.

Having satisfied the demands of the Conservative selection board, Sir Simon began applying for seats, and was soon adopted in Alyn & Deeside. He says:

I was lucky to get selected to fight a seat in north Wales in 1983, which I didn't win – it was a safe Labour seat – [but] the result was good, I got the majority down to 1,368. Between '83 and '87 it was a case of hawking oneself round trying to get selected for a safe Tory seat.

The 'hawking around' paid off, and in 1986, Sir Simon landed the constituency of Chelmsford in Essex. 'I was relieved because I had been selected for a Tory seat,' he says.

The fly in the ointment was that in 1983, which was the Falklands election when [Conservative] MPs' majorities were going through the roof, Chelmsford went from a majority of 6,500 to a Tory majority after three recounts of 378. It was the second most marginal seat in the country against the Liberals and it was the thirteenth most marginal seat in the country against all parties. I got selected ten months before the '87 election and even people in my Association were saying, 'well, you're not going to win the seat'. The Liberal candidate was the deputy leader of the council and he had brought the gap between the Liberals and the Tories from 27,000 to 378. Though I say it myself, I worked extremely hard between April 1986 and polling day '87, and managed to get elected by 7,761. It was fantastic. It was also humbling. The people of Chelmsford had put their trust in me to be a hard-working constituency MP.

Arriving in the House of Commons as an MP in June 1987, Sir Simon found himself at an advantage compared to fellow members of his intake who were new to the place. He says:

I remember on my first day going to the Admission Order Office for some reason, and although there had been a six-year gap between when I stopped working for Sally Oppenheim and becoming an MP, I turned up and the person behind the counter, who had known me when I was last there, the first thing he said was, 'Oh, hello, how nice to see you, who are you working for now?' I had to rather bashfully tell him I was actually a Member of Parliament now. Because I had worked there for six years, I knew the geographical layout of the building, I knew the procedures and everything else.

Sir Simon took to life as an MP 'like a duck to water'. 'There were two things I wanted to do,' he says.

Number one was establish a reputation, hopefully, as a first-class, hard-working constituency MP. Because, and I was aware of this from knocking on doors beforehand in Chelmsford, if you take your constituents for granted, if you become so grounded that you're not interested in your constituents and your constituency, then, potentially, you could lose your seat. I was always aware, the whole time I was there, that the reason I had a wonderful life, I had been a minister, I had met with those, I had done that, was because the people of Chelmsford kept returning me to the House of Commons. In that respect, I was determined that they would get an efficient, fast constituency service, and that I would be around the community, taking part in events and visiting things and everything else that an MP should do.

[Second,] honestly, it would be less than candid for me not to say that I hoped to be a minister as well. That fortunately happened. The whole time I was in Parliament apart from the first two years and a two-year gap between '99 and '01, and then when I ceased to be a minister [in October 2013], I was on the front bench, both in the government and opposition, in one form or another.

From 1989 to 1994, Sir Simon served as a parliamentary private secretary, first to Tim Eggar at the Department for Trade and Industry, and then Gillian Shephard, the Agriculture Secretary, before joining the Whips' Office. He finally became a minister proper in the last year of John Major's government, between 1996 and 1997, when he served as a Health minister.

Like many Conservative MPs who were in Parliament at the time, Sir Simon describes the long opposition years, when New Labour was in government between 1997 and 2010, as a difficult period. 'You can't influence the agenda,' he says.

I remember, it was probably 2001, I was the shadow Minister of Health and I was leading the opposition in committee on a health bill, and I had spotted that there was a typo in the bill, so I tabled an amendment to correct it. They wouldn't give me and the Tories the satisfaction of amending the bill. They said I was absolutely right, it was a typo, and they would amend it on report. It's a very little example, but it's symptomatic of how emasculated and impotent we were in opposition.

It got better when Cameron became leader, particularly after [Gordon] Brown became Prime Minister, because despite the huge hill he had to climb to overturn the major majority, it looked like we did stand a chance to form the next government.

Better times were to follow. While other Conservative MPs found themselves pushed aside to make way for Liberal Democrats when the coalition government was formed following the 2010 general election, Sir Simon found himself promoted from his post as an opposition whip to become a minister at the Department of Health, under the sometimes tumultuous tenure of Andrew Lansley as Secretary of State. Despite David Cameron's promise that there would be no 'top-down reorganisation' of the NHS, Mr Lansley had some radical changes planned – which would stretch the coalition to the limits.

'Cameron rang me up and gave me the job,' Sir Simon says.

It was great. I had been a minister in the '90s, so in that respect it was not new. What was different this time was I was taking through the Commons the Andrew Lansley Health Bill, which was fairly controversial and rather difficult. We had to pause progress following Liberal Democrat spring conference in 2011 where Shirley Williams [Lib Dem peer and founding member of the SDP] and others had got to Nick Clegg [then Deputy Prime Minister and Lib Dem Leader]. We had to have a six-week pause and we made changes as a result of that and we then had to go back into committee to deal with it.

During his second spell at the Department of Health, Sir Simon was also responsible for a social care Bill which put patients and carers in direct control of their budgets, something he describes as his greatest achievement in government.

He is sanguine about the fact that he did not rise to the very top of the ministerial tree, saying:

If I were to become a shadow Cabinet minister or Cabinet minister that would have been great, but up to a point that wasn't up to me. Was I desperately disappointed I didn't get to that level? No. I would have liked to have done, but I wasn't crying in my cups and becoming bitter because it didn't happen.

In 2011, Sir Simon came face to face with one of his political heroes. '[My] best meeting was with Hillary Clinton,' he says.

I was a supporter of Bill Clinton in the 1990s when hardly

any Tory MPs supported [the Clintons]. I worked on Hillary's campaign in 2008. When Obama came for his state visit in '11, she came three days before just to make sure everything was running smoothly. A great friend of mine, Patrick McLoughlin, was the Chief Whip; he had a word with [then Foreign Secretary] William Hague for me to have a meeting with her while she was there. William bumped into me beforehand and said: 'I am going to arrange this meeting for you and Hillary but there is one condition, and he told me what the condition was. And there was no problem with that condition. It was all sorted.

So I turn up, we have our meeting, we chat about New Hampshire where I worked on her campaign, other general things, and then the meeting came to an end. And Hague said: 'OK, Simon? Go on…' And I pulled my sleeve out to show Clinton my Hillary Clinton watch I always wear. And she looked at it and couldn't quite believe what she had seen. She then leaned forward, looked at it again, and shrieked. Secret Service detail took two steps forward and one was heard saying to the other, 'What the hell has he done to her?' She grabbed me by the hand, pulled me along the corridor and down the stairs, out of the building and into the Foreign Office courtyard shouting 'Get me Huma!' And Huma Abedin [Mrs Clinton's aide] was waiting in the car to go, was dragged out of the car, and she said: 'Come here, Huma, come and see Simon's watch.' So I showed her my watch, she politely oohed and ahed over it, and then Hillary said: 'Let's have a photograph looking at the watch.' So photographs were taken of Hillary holding my hand looking at the watch. Then she said, 'We must have a proper photograph done now,' and her hand went across my back and we had an official photograph, which was probably one of the happiest times of my recent life.

In 2013, Sir Simon resigned from the government in order to stand to become Deputy Speaker in the Commons, a move he claims was motivated largely by mischief, a final sally in a deliciously combative feud with the Speaker, John Bercow. He says of his decision to stand for the post of Deputy:

That was just for fun because John Bercow loathed me so much and I wasn't very fond of him. At our first Health Questions when we were in government he annoyed me so much by twice criticising me that I mouthed that he was, 'a stupid, sanctimonious little dwarf', which at the time no one was aware of except for me.

I got back to my departmental office when the private secretary rang through and said that a journalist was on the line, would I take the call? He said to me: 'I can lip read. Was it really "stupid, sanctimonious little dwarf" that you mouthed?' No point in lying about it, so I said 'Yeah', and then all hell broke loose. I kept waiting for No. 10, or the Chief Whip, who was a great friend of mine and who I was having dinner with that night, to get on to me and say, 'you know, you cannot behave like that, you have got to apologise', and it never happened.

I went into work the next morning and my private secretary, who had only known me for a month, was there with a piece of A4 paper, closely typed. She said: 'No. 10 have been on, they want to know are you going to apologise to the Walking with Giants charity about your comments yesterday because they need to know in case it comes up at PMQs.' And I said: 'Who are the Walking with Giants charity?' Because I had never heard of them. And she said, 'Well, they are a charity for people of limited growth. They are outraged. They want a meeting. And an apology.' She said: 'I have got a letter of apology here for you to sign, Minister,' and spontaneously and probably not very cleverly at the time, I immediately took one look at it and said, 'Oh do grow up.' I said, 'Listen, I will apologise to the charity because I don't want them milking this for publicity for the next week or so, but I'm not apologising to Bercow.'

Months after the fuss around Sir Simon's 'dwarf' remark had died down, David Cameron, who also had a somewhat testy relationship with Mr Bercow, reignited the furore with a speech to journalists at the Commons' Press Gallery. Sir Simon takes up the story again:

Apparently he started it by saying: 'Most of you know my Health minister, Simon Burns. What you won't know is that recently his car reversed into the Speaker's car in the Speaker's courtyard. The Speaker was watching this through his window and he came out of Speaker's house screaming at Burns that he was not happy. To which Burns turned around and said: 'Well, which one are you?' The whole thing blew up again, and of course the Walking with Giants people demanded an apology from Cameron. Cameron was Prime Minister, he wasn't the Minister for Health, and so No. 10 turned round to them and said: 'No, no apology, it was a joke.'

Having assumed his last Parliament would run until 2020, Sir Simon had already announced that he was planning to stand down when Theresa May surprised him by going to the country three years early. He had a moment's indecision about whether to stand again, but on the whole is relaxed about leaving the Commons. He spent the general election helping out at Conservative HQ, and says his newfound liberty has been 'wonderful so far'. He has no plans to return to the Commons any time soon. 'There is something sad about ex-MPs wandering around the House of Commons,' he says.

I haven't bothered to get a pass, which I gather I'm entitled to, to go there. I'll miss the people, I'll miss the camaraderie, and I'll miss a lot of the constituents who became friends. I can keep in touch with them in a social way. I won't miss, what in some ways did kill the job for me, the mass-produced campaigning emails by different organisations. Emails and letters from constituents who have got problems are the bread and butter of my job. But the mass-produced bloody emails, organised by 38 Degrees or whoever, it's the same names signing them who never vote Tory, not that that matters in one respect, that did kill part of the job, because it was so predictable.

CV

Born in Nottingham, childhood in Accra, Ghana, and boarding school in Lincolnshire. A political adviser, magazine journalist and researcher at the Institute of Directors.

1983   unsuccessfully contests Alyn & Deeside.
1987   becomes MP for Chelmsford.
1994   becomes government whip.
1996   becomes Health minister.

1997   becomes MP for West Chelmsford, becomes shadow Business minister.

1998   becomes shadow Communities minister.

1999   returns to back benches.

2001   becomes shadow Health minister.

2005   becomes opposition whip.

2010   becomes Health minister.

2012   becomes Transport minister.

2013   unsuccessfully stands as deputy Speaker, returns to back benches.

2015   appointed Knight Bachelor.

2017   stands down from Parliament.

Divorced with two children.

DAME ANGELA
WATKINSON

D ame Angela Watkinson, 75, was Conservative MP
for Upminster 2001–10 and Hornchurch & Upminster 2010–17.

How did you end up in Parliament?

'I was a whole generation older than most candidates.
Nobody ever remarked on it. And I went through the
whole approval process, came out the other side after the
dreaded weekend and found myself an approved candidate. And so I applied for Upminster where I had lived
for over thirty years and knew it like the back of my hand
and was selected, and we won the seat back from Labour
in 2001.'

How did you feel on first becoming an MP?

'I did settle in very quickly. The one thing I have never encountered throughout the entire process down here is any gender prejudice at all. I think I learned when I was at work that people treat you the way you allow them to treat you, and I have never tolerated being talked down to, and I think people just don't dare do it.'

Best of times:

'I think if I'm honest I enjoyed the Whips' Office most. There is a camaraderie in there, it's almost like an extended family, very supportive. It's being at the hub of government, at the very centre, which I really liked.'

Worst of times:

'My lowest point happened almost immediately after arriving in 2001, over the debates on the Iraq War. I was told by the Prime Minister on three separate occasions from the despatch box that the United Kingdom was in danger of attack from weapons of mass destruction in forty-five minutes. And as a very naive new Member, I thought it must be true. If the Prime Minister is saying it at the despatch box, however incredible it seems, it must be true. I realised later that it wasn't. And I felt really bad about that; really bad.'

Why are you leaving?

'I thought to commit for another five years would probably be unwise because if I did another five years that would take me to eighty-one, which I think is probably too old. I know some people do stay on into their eighties but I thought, I am going to have a few years where I am well enough to do things and to have the time to do them.'

What are your thoughts for future MPs?

'People set great store by talking, but I think listening is even more important, particularly talking to your constituents and local businesses, charities, and the public services. Really listen to them because then you know how policy is affecting them and how it might be improved. When somebody tells you something, ask yourself two questions; one is: is this true? And the second one is: why do they want me to think this? If you are a truthful person, you just assume that other people are. But sadly life isn't like that so you do [have to] delve behind what people are telling you.'

Do you have any regrets about leaving the Commons? And what are you going to do next?

'Yes, I shall miss all my colleagues. I shall have some holidays, because although I have been to almost every corner of the globe as an MP, you don't really see much of the country. You spend most of your time in meetings and in international hotels, which could be pretty much anywhere, they're all the same. There are a lot of places I would like to go back to and actually have the time be a tourist. So I will do that, but I am going to find something to do. I can't just do nothing.'

DAME ANGELA WATKINSON: THE FULL STORY

Dame Angela Watkinson entered politics late in life, having taken years to build up the courage to get involved. Her parents came from diametrically opposite sides of the political divide. Her father was an old-school socialist and her mother, at heart, a Tory. Dame Angela was clear from an early age that she was, by 'instinct', a Conservative. She says:

I came from a poor, working-class family living in the East End of London. I used to listen to the adults around me, this was in the days when children used to listen when adults were talking, and they were always complaining about 'them' and 'they'. I got the idea that whoever these people were, and I had no idea, they obviously were held responsible for everything, blamed for everything, and they also got to make all the decisions. I couldn't understand why people, my family, were content just to sit back and complain, because if they thought that 'they' were getting it wrong, why didn't they do it themselves if they thought they could do it better? And I think from a very early age, I had this germ of an idea that whoever 'they' were, I wanted to be one of them.

It was in the days when there was an exam called the 11-plus, which I passed, so went to the grammar school in the neighbouring town – Wanstead County School, it was called. It was quite a cultural shock, because I came face to face with children from middle-class families and they owned their own homes, their fathers had cars, and they had fridges and telephones. It was like another planet to me.

My father, who was old Labour, didn't want me to mix with the other children in case it gave me ideas above my station. But my mother, I realise now, was a Conservative, and a visionary, and she almost wanted to relive her life through me because she hadn't had the opportunity [to prosper]. She pushed me very hard, harder than was comfortable a lot of the time. My father was bitterly resentful of anyone who was doing better than him in life. It never occurred to him that they might have worked very hard and earned it. He always felt it must be in some way undeserved. Whereas my mother [taught me] one of the first lessons I learned in life: if you want something there is only one way to get it and that's to work hard, which I did.

And she also taught me personal financial management.

There used to be a little silver coin called a sixpence, and I used to have one of those as my pocket money every week, but I had to save a penny of it. The first half of the year, it was to buy ice cream in the summer holidays, the second half was to buy Christmas presents.

I have never been in debt in my life, apart from the mortgage – that's the only debt I have ever had. I think like a lot of people who are working-class in origin, I have a horror of that. So I have always made sure that however modest my finances work, I lived within them. That was a very valuable lesson my mother taught me, I think. My father was hopeless though.

Pushed by her mother's desire to live vicariously through her, Dame Angela did well at school. 'I think I am living proof that grammar schools give opportunity and ambition and aspiration to children from disadvantaged backgrounds,' she says.

The only thing was, they couldn't afford for me to go to university, so I had to leave school at sixteen and I went to work in a bank. And it was much later, when I had three teenage children and a full-time job, that I completed my education on day release. That was quite a challenge, but I do like challenges.

By now, Dame Angela had also begun to take an interest in politics, but found it difficult to imagine becoming a full-time politician. It was not until she was in her forties in the 1980s that she even became a member of the Conservative Party. She says:

I remember when my children were very little, I used to get Conservative literature through the door, and they invited me to go to GMs [general meetings] and things, and I used to think: 'I couldn't possibly go because everybody there will be terribly important.' It was only later that I realised that they were desperate for people to go and help. So it was a very gradual process for me. It wasn't until my children were in their teens that I suddenly got the bit between my teeth and decided that I was a going to become a councillor and then a county councillor.

After a career in banking and local government, I took early retirement and straightaway was elected to Havering Borough Council. I had been working in local government and I used to observe council meetings and think, 'I could do that,' or, 'I could do that better.' And so I got myself elected to Havering Borough Council, and then subsequently to Essex County Council.

In enterprising fashion, having decided a few years later

that she wanted to become an MP, Dame Angela simply applied to Conservative Central Office. She says:

By the time I knew I wanted to be a Member of Parliament, everybody told me I had left it far too late. Because I had no idea how one went about it, I first approached the Candidates' Department. I was aged fifty-seven and everybody said, 'Oh you are far too old, you won't even get a response.' But to their surprise, nobody ever commented on my age.

Dame Angela was lucky – her local constituency, Upminster in Essex, had fallen vacant around the time she had been approved as a candidate. Once a safe Conservative seat, Upminster had fallen to the Labour Party in Tony Blair's landslide of 1997. Dame Angela was determined to win it back. She says:

I don't think I was optimistic – I was hopeful. What I wanted to be sure of was that the day after the election, if I had been beaten, I wouldn't have been beaten if only I had done a bit more. So I made sure that I couldn't possibly have tried any harder. I was selected in 1999 and I worked the seat full time. I was a county councillor at the time and they said, 'We want you to win that seat; so long as you come in for full council, we will excuse you all other duties.' I treated it like a full-time job and went out campaigning all day, every day, for two years. And I won it back with a majority of 1,242, which is imprinted on my memory.

By now, Dame Angela's children had grown up and left home. She found they were nonplussed by her new career as a politician. 'To be honest, they weren't very interested,' she says.

I was out there on my own. Throughout my career they have been mildly interested, that's about as far as it goes. They were all independent and had left home. I did have that very helpful opportunity to use as much time as I liked, because my family were no longer dependent. How women with young children do it, I don't know. I am really full of admiration [at] how they divide themselves between family responsibilities and their jobs, and [election] campaigns in particular, because it was demanding.

Arriving in the House of Commons in June 2001, Dame Angela quickly made herself at home.

The first day, when I came up the steps of St Stephens, the police had obviously looked at all the mug shots and made sure they recognised the new people as they came in.

I knew we hadn't had many gains that year [but] I was very impressed by that.

I knew what [Parliament] was like. I had been up [to Westminster] on numerous occasions. Having been a councillor and county councillor, I knew about meeting discipline and debate, that sort of thing, the structure, except I knew it would be bigger. I have never, ever experienced any gender prejudice at all in the party or parliamentary debates.

Within a few months of arriving in the Commons, in September 2001, Dame Angela witnessed the shocking 9/11 terror attacks at extremely close hand. She says:

I was in Washington DC with the British American Parliamentary Group. We were having a guided tour of the Senate chamber, and we were all having our group photograph taken, and the police came in shouting, 'Get out of the building, go, go, go'. It was like an Arnold Schwarzenegger film. We ran down these marble staircases and our escort said: 'I don't know what's happened but it's obviously something serious.' And then we were all running across the lawn and by that time the news had got through about what had happened at the Twin Towers.

We saw smoke coming up from the [Pentagon]. The whole city just closed down and we couldn't get out.

The Metro had stopped running, all traffic had stopped and the roads were all closed and there were just military aircraft in the air. Everyone gathered around television screens and were standing with their jaws dropped because it was so shocking.

But what I remember of that was that all Americans just came together, whether they were Hispanic or African or Italian or Irish, whatever sort of American they were, they became one. I have got goose pimples thinking about it. People were gathered in hotels and restaurants everywhere, just staring in shock at the television.

We couldn't be reunited with our minibus so we had to walk a very long way around. I saw the brownstone houses you see in the films. Eventually we got to Pennsylvania Avenue and all the flags were at half-mast. We walked up to the British Embassy, and they said, 'You can't go anywhere, there are no internal flights, there are no international flights. You are just going to have to go back to the hotel and wait and see.' It happened on a Tuesday. Eventually, on the Thursday, we were sent home in an RAF TriStar from Andrews Air Force Base. We got into Brize Norton and managed to get into Westminster on the Friday. There was a national day of mourning.

To our amazement, we were then asked to go back to complete our tour. I can remember getting into Dulles airport and the security was really high, as you can imagine.

There was great consternation because my passport showed that I was in the United States, so how was I trying to get in? Because we had gone out through an Air Force base and there was no passport checking. It took a bit of explaining. It was an absolutely amazing trip when we went back. It was the one topic of conversation everywhere. Americans, I think, until that point, had been quite insular and suddenly they were part of the wider world and as vulnerable as everybody else.

The depleted state of the Conservative parliamentary party during the New Labour era meant there were opportunities for advancement early on. Not long after her memorable experience in Washington DC, Dame Angela found her political home in the Commons, the place she would stay on and off for more than a decade. 'I went into the Whips' Office after about six months,' she says. 'I was actually a whip for about ten years. I absolutely loved it, because it's organisation and management, which I'm good at, and I have also got, I think, quite good interpersonal skills, and so I was ideally suited to that role.'

While she enjoyed the work, the turn of the century was not a good time to be a Conservative whip. 'We used to lose by about 100 votes every night,' Dame Angela says.

It was quite depressing. You knew it was going to happen

and there was nothing for it, but you had to try and keep morale up and hope for better times, which did come eventually.

I did enjoy the Whips' Office very much. I came out for a while and I was a shadow minister for early years education. I spent quite a lot of time studying early years education in Sweden, where my son and family live. They are particularly good at it over there. I was also shadow minister for fire and rescue service. I have had several firefighters in my family and it was very helpful to have the day-to-day experience from them as compared to how policy was being developed in Parliament. And also I was shadow Minister for Homelessness for a while. They were very interesting [posts].

Dame Angela was returned to the Whips' Office by David Cameron in 2005, and, when the Conservatives formed the coalition government with the Liberal Democrats, she received the formal title of Lords Commissioner. In reality, she was now an assistant whip, but there were plenty of ceremonial duties involved, including garden parties at Buckingham Palace, which she came to relish. She says:

Being an MP does open doors for you. You meet people you wouldn't otherwise meet and visit places you wouldn't otherwise visit, so it has given me a wealth of memories.

The Queen always invites new Members of Parliament to a reception at Buckingham Palace. I hadn't really expected to see her – if I caught a glimpse of her across the room that would be the most [I could have expected]. But there was quite a big team from the Royal Family out, and they were talking to people, and I remember the Queen talking to me and I just said something incredibly stupid, which I hope lots of other people do. I wanted the floor to open up and swallow me. I had recently read Sue Townsend's book called *The Queen and I*, and [there was a section about the carpets] in Buckingham Palace, which the Queen had to take with her, and the carpet fitter had to chop them up to fit in to the house that they moved into. I just remember standing on the carpets in the reception area and wondering [aloud] if these were the … carpets I had been reading about. The next time I went I made sure that if she should speak to me, I would have something sensible to say, so the communication went very well.

There was one wonderful occasion at the Guildhall, the 400th anniversary of the first Lord Commissioners. In those days, they were allowed to deposit government funds in their own personal bank accounts overnight and keep the interest, so it was a highly prized, desirable job. Certainly that practice has been discontinued. All living Prime Ministers and Chancellors and Lords Commissioners were there and it really was a lovely occasion.

While Dame Angela says she enjoyed being a shadow minister, she will for ever at heart be a whip, and is content that her time in the Commons was largely spent out of sight. 'Other people came and went and I was still there,' she says of her long years in the Whips' Office. Disappointingly, she denies knowledge of the infamous little black book of secrets whips are said to hold as ammunition over potentially rebellious MPs. 'It's so sad to shoot that story down in flames but it really doesn't exist,' Dame Angela says.

There are all sorts of myths about the Whips' Office which people love to tell, but most of them are just that. The one thing about the Whips' Office is confidentiality, so even if there were some interesting goings-on in there, I wouldn't disclose them. That would be dreadful. One or two ex-whips have done that, and written books, but that is really frowned on. Once a whip always a whip. Loyalty is prized above everything.

By 2012, Dame Angela was ready to return to the back benches and no longer desired ministerial office. 'In recent years I thought my energy levels weren't as good as they had been ten years ago,' she says. 'It was better to let the younger, keener ones do it.'

While she gained a reputation as an independent

thinker, attempting from the back benches to air socially Conservative views on subjects such as abortion, she has little regard for parliamentary devices such as Early Day Motions and Private Members Bills.

One thing I would do if I had the power would be ban Early Day Motions,' she says. 'There are about 3,000 each year, and all they do is form a statement of opinion of one MP and then other people who agree and then their names. But members of the public who have a special interest in that subject will be encouraged to think that something is going to happen and it very rarely does. So they raise expectations unrealistically. Private Members Bills are the same. I remember being number two on the order paper one Friday, and the government didn't want number one [to pass], so it was filibustered the entire morning. I didn't even get on. And that happened a lot. It's an awful lot of work and your chances of success are extremely thin.

While she had hoped to serve until 2020, Dame Angela had actually come close to standing down even before Theresa May called the unexpectedly early election for June 2017. She says:

I have had some ill health over the past year and up until Christmas I thought, I'm never going to be able to go back.

But then I really picked up in the early part of this year. Everyone was called in for the Brexit votes, and I managed that fine. I thought I would come back after Easter; and on my very first official day back, I got halfway on the train, and the election was announced.

Interestingly, just as no one made any comment about my age when I joined, similarly no one has commented on my age when I'm retiring. I have had lots of lovely letters from constituents and organisations, people I have dealt with, and nobody has commented. I was expecting people to say, 'Well, it was about time you went.' Nobody has. I have a very nice young woman who is taking over from me. She is new so she will bring her own ideas. She may do something completely different from the way I have.

Dame Angela is not yet sure what she will do with her time, but is determined that she is not retiring altogether. 'There may be a couple of directorships,' she says.

I don't want to make any hasty decisions. I will wait until the election is over and then I'll decide. It's quite strange to wake up in the morning and think I haven't got to go anywhere, nobody is expecting me anywhere. It's quite a novel feeling. I'm not sure I quite like it. I have got to do something. I can't sit at home watching daytime television.

CV

Born in Leytonstone, Essex. A banker and local government official.

2001   elected MP for Upminster.

2002   becomes opposition whip.

2004   becomes shadow Education minister.

2005   becomes shadow Communities minister, becomes opposition whip.

2010   elected MP for Hornchurch & Upminster, becomes government whip.

2012   returns to back benches.

2013   appointed a Dame Commander.

2017   stands down from Parliament.

Married to Roy, three children.

DOUGLAS CARSWELL

Douglas Carswell, 46, was Conservative MP for Harwich 2005–10, Conservative MP for Clacton 2010–14, UK Independence Party MP for Clacton 2014–17, and Independent MP for Clacton 2017.

How did you end up in Parliament?
'I felt very strongly [that] we need[ed] to get out of the EU, and I thought the Conservative Party would be the vehicle to make it happen.'

How did you feel on first becoming an MP?
'Everyone was terribly friendly. There was a sense of excitement and exhilaration, and the first few months were a rather wonderful feeling. [However,] I became disillusioned

with the Commons very quickly. After about six months, a year, I started to think: "It's fixed, it's a cartel."'

Best of times:
'The MPs' expenses scandal was very traumatic for many MPs, but actually I found it woke the place up. People started to realise that it was essentially parasitic.'

Worst of times:
'There was a moment about six months to a year after I got in where I thought: "This is going to be an appalling waste of time for everyone." You have got to remember, David Cameron and George Osborne were leading the opposition; politics seemed like a game where clever-clever PPE graduates from Oxbridge [were in charge].'

Why are you leaving?
'I came into politics because I wanted us to leave the European Union. Once the Prime Minister of the United Kingdom said that we were going to trigger the process to get us out, I said, "job done". It was very straightforward. There is no complexity in it. I'm just glad it only took twelve years not twenty-something years.'

What are your thoughts for future MPs?
'We live in an age of anti-politics, so don't ever do the

party stuff. Remember the folks who voted for you. Ultimately, they, not the Tory whips, not the people you meet in the [Commons] tea room, are the folks who put you where you are. You will sleep easy at night if you keep them happy. If you do stuff that makes them unhappy, it doesn't matter what you do in the Commons, it will end in failure. And [have] a bit of humility too. Twenty years ago, the Blairites thought they were invincible. Look at them now.'

Do you have any regrets about leaving the Commons? And what are you going to do next?

'I've stood in five elections, I've only ever lost to Tony Blair, and I was helpful in a referendum. Why would I want to hang around? I don't want to sound unkind, but that's absolutely right.

I've got lots and lots of interests totally unrelated to politics. The beauty of not being a public figure any more is I don't have to talk about my private life in public. I'm leaving public life, and going off to do things completely unrelated to frontline politics. I feel very good about it.'

DOUGLAS CARSWELL: THE FULL STORY

For Douglas Carswell it has always been about Europe. It was what drove him into politics in the first place, and he leaves Parliament following the EU referendum with a sense of mission accomplished. He was born and brought up in Uganda, arriving in the UK in his teens to go to boarding school. His childhood in Africa informed his deep love for Great Britain – and his consequent distaste for Europe. 'What [should] they know of England who only England know?' he says, quoting Kipling. 'I grew up in Uganda and I think I always had an appreciation of what is so special about Britain. It is an extraordinarily successful country in so many ways, and yet the European Union is so obviously bad.'

It wasn't until Mr Carswell was at the University of East Anglia that his interest in politics, and particularly politics as it related to what he describes as the 'historic forty-year mistake over Europe', began to develop. For him, Euroscepticism came first, Conservativism second. He says:

It was really the Maastricht Treaty that made me first be aware of having political opinions. When I was at university and the government signed the Maastricht Treaty, I remember thinking it was pretty extraordinary and I began to form an interest in politics.

The idea that you can by grand design [manage] things centrally, it seems so obviously a bad idea. I remember being baffled that anyone could possibly think that the euro would be a success. The idea that you could make a success of the European continent by running it through an unelected technocracy is so obviously a daft idea.

I genuinely believe that this is the greatest country on earth. We can do better than having third rate, grubby mediocrities from John Major on thinking that we can't do things. Why do we have such a low regard that we can't regulate our own affairs? It struck me as a bizarre.

Today people are baffled that we thought it was a good idea to be in the European Union and part of the euro. I always thought it was an odd way to do things. It proved to be a historic anomaly.

As he became more involved politically, Mr Carswell got to know other Eurosceptic student politicians, including Daniel Hannan, the future MEP and leading Leave campaigner. Mr Carswell says:

He had formed Campaign for an Independent Britain, and I got involved with that. We talked a lot about the tactics for making it happen, but, realistically, the vehicle for getting us out [was that] we needed to have a Conservative majority, and a majority of the Conservatives in the House [of Commons] in favour.

While employed in investment management, Mr Carswell decided to step up his political activism by standing for

Parliament in the 2001 general election. His choice of a constituency was challenging to say the least, but would have a 'profound' impact on his life. He says: 'I first started in 2001 in Sedgefield against Tony Blair, and I'm afraid I came second, but I loved it so much doing that I thought: 'Gosh, I could do this.'

Tony Blair was the Prime Minister, and I got so fed up with people complaining about Tony Blair and how dreadful he was, I thought I need to stand against him myself.

I managed to get a pretty good swing. I think I'm right in saying I'm the only person who's ever stood against Tony Blair who managed to reduce his majority. Against pretty much everybody else it went up.

I rather enjoyed it. I took it very seriously. I pretty much knocked on every door in the constituency over the course of about a year.

I learnt the importance of humility in politics. It's a fact that we all forget now, but Blair in his heyday was actually a very formidable politician. I remember being very impressed. He knew people in the constituency at a very micro-level and he was brilliant at remembering [everyone]. He had a way with talking with people that was exceptional. People often talk about Bill Clinton, well Blair was as good [as] Bill Clinton.

One never meets anyone who remembers voting for

him these days, but at the time he made me realise that we as the blue team simply couldn't compete with the Blairite Labour Party because they were so good. In their lowest moments in the '80s they had clearly realised they were out of touch and they had done something about it.

And it made me realise that maybe the Tory modernisers were on to something. After the 2001 election I started to realise that to be capable of winning a seat, one had to learn some of the lessons from the other side. I learnt things that I put to good use in practice. I only won my Clacton seat [in 2005] by 920 votes. I think if I had not have learned that hyper-local, very personalised approach up in Sedgefield [I might not have won].

The Sedgefield experience also got Mr Carswell thinking more deeply about politics as it was being offered by his party to electorates outside of the home counties. He says:

I remember asking myself: what is it that makes people in that part of the country who are traditionally Labour supporters, the blue-collar Labour base, always support a Labour elite like Blair who doesn't share their values?

I started to think the way to sever the Labour base from the Labour elite is through direct democracy and the use of directly elected police chiefs, police and crime commissioners, the use of referenda, the use of recall and open primary elections.

It was after 2001, the experience of standing in Sedgefield, that I published a paper called 'Direct Democracy: Empowering People to Improve their Lives'. It was basically an attempt to sketch out ideas for the centre-right, to try to drive a wedge between the liberal left elite and the blue-collar base. I'm pleased to say that it seems to have yielded some success. The referendum seems to have helped do that; all those police and crime commissioners elected certainly don't share a liberal left agenda on justice.

Mr Carswell emerged from his experience in Sedgefield determined to become an MP. He drew closer to the Conservative Party, finding work at its London headquarters – where he first came into contact with the future Prime Minister David Cameron, and several current Cabinet ministers. He says: 'I worked in the Conservative research department, reporting to Greg Clark and one D. Cameron of all people; two of the brightest people I've ever come across; privilege to work for them.'

Mr Carswell now set about finding himself a constituency to fight ahead of the 2005 general election. The one he landed, Clacton in Essex, was again not an easy option. 'I didn't get a safe seat,' he says.

Labour had won it in 1997 and increased their majority in 2001.

We now live in a world where the Tories will almost certainly win in Clacton with more than half the vote ... but it didn't look like that in the run-up to a 2005 election. I remember thinking that everyone assumes this is going to be unwinnable, actually I think I can do it.

But before he could concentrate on winning Clacton at the general election, he had to be selected. Again, it came down to Europe.

There was a very, very competitive selection process. I was asked by the couple of hundred Conservative activists in Clacton Town Hall if there was anything else to say, and I said to them: 'Look, I am absolutely serious when I say that we need to leave the European Union. I don't just believe it, I will do absolutely everything I can as your Member of Parliament to get us out of the EU. I am absolutely serious about that.' I think I won the selection by a couple of votes. That was very key to me getting selected.

Given the challenge he faced to win his seat, Mr Carswell was unimpressed with the offering presented by the national party. 'In the run up to the 2005 election it was very touch and go as to whether we would get a majority in Clacton,' he says. 'We were completely hamstrung by the disastrous consequences of [the leadership's] thinking on Europe. It made all those other promises that a centre-right government ought to make rather implausible. It was a great gamble. I thought there was a 50/50 chance.'

The gamble paid off – thanks to his hard work. Mr Carswell was elected with a majority of fewer than 1,000 votes. Waiting for the result was nerve-racking. He says:

I don't know if you know what 950 votes looks like when it's piled up, but it's only a few inches. There was this long table in the middle of the hall, and they piled my pile of paper in a row, and my closest rival's paper, and it was neck and neck until the last minute. It was very, very close. Enormous relief when I won. It was exhilarating.

I made a point of not cheering and gloating and not trying to behave like a triumphalist politician, because I was very, very conscious from the word go that I had a very slender majority and by definition most people hadn't voted for me. Although I had won, from the beginning I thought: I need to maintain that slight air of humility. I was starting to appreciate the mood of anti-politics.

Mr Carswell's arrival in Westminster was an enjoyable experience. 'It was a fantastic first few months,' he says. 'I went and sought advice from MPs I knew were highly respected in their constituencies and I learnt from what they had been doing.' The feeling did not last. From the beginning, as he contemplated his mission to work towards extracting the UK from the European Union, he realised he was virtually a lone voice in the House of Commons of the day.

He says: 'I compiled a list soon after I arrived in Westminster of all the MPs we could count on who agreed that we should leave the EU. I think we got as far as twelve. So I realised that on that issue one was in a tiny minority.'

But it wasn't just on the EU that Mr Carswell found himself out of step with most of his MP colleagues. He says:

I started to realise that on many of the macro issues of the day, it was run as a consensus between the two front benches, and the usual channels rigged things so that a lot of the disagreements were actually quite theatrical, under licence. There was something quite bogus about it.

I remember being particularly outraged by something the Speaker did. We were trying to frustrate the Labour government on some Europe issue, and we got some Labour people, the Labour rebels, to table some amendments they could support, so that instead of having a dozen or two dozen Tory rebels in the lobby, we would hopefully have Labour supporters in there too. And the

Speaker didn't select the amendments when it was obvious to me that the Speaker should select them because they would test the government's position.

I remember thinking, 'The whole thing is useless. Parliament has lost its purpose. There is no point being here.' Parliament was pretty pointless and support for leaving the EU tiny.

Out of step with the Conservative leadership over Europe, and prepared to be a serial rebel on the issue, Mr Carswell was aware from the outset that he and his Eurosceptic colleagues were unlikely ever to have a career on the front bench. He says:

This tiny group of us waged this unrelenting campaign [over Europe]. It meant that we forsook any chance of any promotion. I realised from before I ever got in[to the House of Commons] that in politics you can either write the script or be the actor. You can either be something in terms of office or do something in terms of change. You can rarely do both.

I realised that in order to make the party move in a direction it had to move, I would, to put it modestly, have to exhaust whatever capital and goodwill there was towards me fairly quickly.

The system is almost designed to filter out anyone who

doesn't deal in obsequiousness. Almost a prerequisite of getting promoted is to show subservience to the group-think. Some of the clever ones conceal their ability to think independently, but [with] most of them, I am afraid, that obsequiousness is authentic.

So frustrated was Mr Carswell with the way Parliament operated that as his first term drew to a close he had all but made his mind up to stand down at the 2010 general election. Then something happened which shook the place up: the MPs' expenses scandal, which hit the Commons like a whirlwind in the spring of 2009. When it emerged that the Speaker, Michael Martin, and his committee of senior backbenchers had been attempting to block the publication of what turned out to be evidence of the egregious abuse of the expenses system, he was spurred to action.

Mr Carswell said:

I didn't mean to be a rebellious sort but I thought: 'We need to get rid of the Speaker.' Not just because of the response to the MPs' expenses scandal and attempts to fight [the] dissemination of information, but because what you might call the 'usual channels', the old boys' system, is wrong. I found renewed energy in tabling the motion to get rid of the Speaker, and then pushing that whole agenda of saying we need a Speaker who makes life difficult, who restores purpose, who tables loads of questions. And then [John] Bercow took over. And I actually started enjoying it again once Bercow took over because there was a purpose in Parliament again, there was a chance of tripping up the government if they got things wrong.

The rules were no longer stacked against us.

As well as the arrival of a new Speaker, Mr Carswell was energised by a series of reforms which were introduced following a review by the Labour backbencher Tony Wright, which included: 'allowing the back benches to have some say over the House of Commons agenda'. Mr Carswell adds:

That allowed us to table a substantive motion demanding a referendum [on the EU], which is what finally pushed Cameron into agreeing to a referendum, in October 2011.

All those changes began to take effect and [the Commons] started to work properly for me. Until that point, up until Bercow came along, the best you could hope for would be to ingratiate yourself with someone on the frontbench team. Once you could actually do the job of holding the government to account, regardless of whether you were in opposition or they were the government, you could actually do your job as a member of the legislature. It began to become interesting again.

Armed with the tools the Wright reforms gave him, Mr Carswell set about using his second term in office to attempt to force the new coalition government, headed by David Cameron, to agree to a referendum on British membership of the EU. He says of his actions:

It was always with a view to the question of getting us out of the European Union. When I first wrote my columns to check, there were fewer than a dozen MPs who one could count on to support that. So the first aim was to popularise the idea of a referendum.

Cameron had at various points to concede the principle. He had given in, in opposition, on the idea of a referendum on the Lisbon Treaty, gave a cast iron guarantee, and then reneged on it. We used every conceivable trick in the book, every conceivable device, to wage this absolutely unrelenting guerrilla war and finally he had to concede that we would have a referendum. The key moment was when eighty-plus Tory MPs, 111 MPs in total, defied a three-line whip. That marked the moment when he stopped trying to oppose the holding of a referendum on Europe in principle.

Mr Carswell was determined to hold the Prime Minister's feet to the fire to force him to follow through on his promise to hold a referendum. As he detected what he sensed was a wavering in Mr Cameron's resolve, Mr Carswell decided he needed to keep the pressure on by bolstering the still relatively obscure UK Independence Party. He defected to UKIP, and October 2014 triggered what he intended to be a high-profile by-election to ensure the issue of the EU remained high in the public's perception.

Mr Carswell says of Mr Cameron:

He conceded the principle, and then he clearly started to renege on that, and that's when I thought, 'Do you know what, I'm only really fundamentally in politics to get us out of the EU. My career is worth the risk of calling a by-election if that helps force him to honour his promises.'

I left the Conservatives and called a by-election for two reasons that were very, very clear in my mind: one was that, because he had been backtracking, to make absolutely certain we got the referendum; [the second was] to make absolutely certain that we got the right people running the [referendum] campaign.

Having achieved his first aim of forcing the Prime Minister to keep his promise to hold a referendum, Mr Carswell now set about his second. He was concerned that UKIP was too dominated by 'fruit cakes and loonies', in Mr Cameron's memorable phrase, to have credibility, and he hoped that by joining it he could lend the party some much-needed authority. It was the start of what would become an infamous and long-running feud with Nigel Farage, the iconoclastic UKIP leader, about the way the party presented itself to the public.

Mr Carswell says:

A small group of us started to look at some data in 2011, 2012, and we started to realise that when the worst sort of Eurosceptics dominated the news media, support for leaving went down. We realised that the Downing Street game was to give us the referendum, but to make sure it was a Cameron versus Farage narrative, which is why I think they were willing to concede it. A Cameron versus Farage, they think they would have won – and I think they would have won.

As the years passed and his skirmishes with Mr Farage intensified, Mr Carswell admits that he began to despair of making UKIP more palatable to the wider electorate.

He says:

Well if it was [my aim], it wasn't a wholly successful initiative. I had hoped that support for leaving the EU and Euroscepticism wouldn't be synonymous with UKIP, and when people thought UKIP they wouldn't just think of a certain kind of 'kipper'. After the general election of 2015,

I came to the realisation that UKIP was such a toxic brand that the aim should be not to try to influence anyone's perception of UKIP but to make sure actually UKIP was kept well away from the referendum campaign. And on that we succeeded. Just. It was very close, but we did it.

As a leading member of the Leave campaign, Mr Carswell concentrated on ensuring that politicians of all parties were presented to the public, arguing the case for quitting the EU.

Mr Carswell is aware that the resulting success for Leave in the June 2016 EU referendum now has many authors. He is content with his own small place in history. 'I've achieved what I achieved; I'm absolutely thrilled with the outcome,' he says.

David Cameron once said to me at PMQs [Prime Minister's Questions] that I should get a sense of humour; I've been laughing myself silly since 23 June last year.

I've been absolutely thrilled. If you had said to me when I first stood in 2001 that within sixteen years we would be leaving the EU, I simply would not have believed it possible.

In 2005 when I made that list of true believers, it was terrifyingly small. I had said during the [2005 Clacton election] campaign that we should leave the EU; it had become front page in a Sunday newspaper and I had had a call from a Tory official rebuking me and threatening me. Soon after I arrived [in the Commons], a couple of whips took me to the side and explained I should forget all of that if I wanted to get on. I am absolutely thrilled that now one of those whips is a minister who is working on making Brexit happen. A beautiful sight to behold. But of course, the wonderful thing about politics is that politicians always rewrite their own memories. In order to win that campaign, it was necessary to allow people to think it was their idea all along.

Mr Carswell has still not recovered from the high of the referendum result. 'It was the culmination of my political career,' he says.

I thought we were going to win but I wasn't certain. I had discussed it with my wife a couple of weeks before the referendum. We agreed that I wouldn't stand again, and I thought that if we won the referendum I would leave politics with a smile; if we lost I would go away in a huff.

The events of that night are etched on his memory. He says:

I had some data in my pocket when I was being interviewed

by the BBC. It was live [and] I had a breakdown of the early results, what they would need to be if abrogated on a national level in order for us to win. I think Nottingham and Sunderland came in and I said to [then Energy Secretary] Amber Rudd after the cameras stopped rolling: 'I think we've done it'. Amber is a wonderful person. I have got a lot of time for her. She played a straight bat.

With every set of results that came in, we were getting more confident. By the time the final result came in, I was at the Vote Leave HQ and Dan Hannan and [Vote Leave director] Dominic Cummings gave these beautiful speeches standing on top of a desk. I was absolutely exhausted, physically exhausted, but I couldn't sleep I was so happy.

As far as Mr Carswell is concerned, once Britain had voted to leave the EU there was no longer any point to his remaining in Parliament. He also saw no reason to stay a member of the increasingly dysfunctional UKIP. He quit the party the following March, once Theresa May had signed Article 50 of the Lisbon Treaty which triggered the formal start of the two-year Brexit process.

He says:

I had very nearly announced that I was going to leave UKIP, or leave politics, on 24 June [2016]. Several people said to me, 'Hang in there, just wait, we don't know if there's going to be a serious rear-guard action by the Remainiacs to try to subvert the results.' Then there was [the] whole Gina Miller thing [the legal challenge forcing a Commons vote on the Brexit negotiations]. Some people said one still needs UKIP being around to put fear into the Labour Party. And so I hung on as long as I could.

For me the key point was triggering Article 50. As soon as Article 50 was triggered, I thought 'job done'.

Before he left UKIP, there was a final messy row with Mr Farage over his refusal to take up additional funding which the party's vote share entitled him to, which the party leader wanted to utilise for campaigning. Mr Carswell denies that he wanted to replace Mr Farage as leader, and says that his motives first for joining and then leaving UKIP were always about one thing: quitting the EU.

It's one of those really weird things in politics: so often if you say to people you want to do something, and you say to them why you are doing it, they will always, always, always look for ulterior motives.

I'm not leadership material. It's not my forte. I have a grudging admiration for all party leaders. To be a party leader, it's unrelenting, thankless, it's brutal. I just don't have the patience to do it. To be a party leader, whether you're

Tim Farron or Nigel Farage or Theresa May, you have to have huge reserves of patience with other people. I hope I have enough self-awareness to know that it would be bad for me and bad for any party that I led. It's not my thing.

In his final few weeks in Parliament, Mr Carswell sat as an independent. For a time, there was a suggestion that he might return to the Conservative fold. But although he campaigned on behalf of Theresa May during the general election, he says he was not tempted to rejoin the Tories, even in its newly Eurosceptic guise.

He says of his final days in the Commons:

It was a wonderful end, actually. I felt at my most comfortable being an independent. I'm not really a very good Conservative. I've got a lot of admiration for the Conservative Party [but] I like change, I don't like conserving things.

The Tory Party had to pivot. In the 1930s, they were totally wrong on the issue of appeasement, then under pressure they pivoted and in the space of a few months, everyone forgot that they were in favour of appeasement and everyone remembered that they had always been in favour of rearmament. And then in the 1970s they were almost all on completely the wrong side of the economic debate, they were Keynesians. Then the IMF forced the

Labour Party to become monetarists, and the Tory Party all became monetarists. By the mid-1980s it was impossible to find a Tory who hadn't always been a natural Thatcherite.

And what we are witnessing [now] is like that. For forty years the Tory Party was on the wrong side of the Europe question. We are seeing the pivot. Some people would say it's shameless, I would say it's wonderful pragmatism.

I'm not a flagrant sycophantic supporter of Theresa May by any stretch, but supporting her in [the general] election is the easiest decision I've had to make.

Like everyone else, Mr Carswell was surprised by Mrs May's announcement of an early general election, but he was clear about what he wanted to do.

'I thought I had got maybe two years to make the transition from being an MP to life outside,' he says.

I choreographed in my mind that I would announce leaving UKIP when Article 50 was triggered, and announce leaving Parliament when we actually left [the EU] in 2019.

All the [general election] announcement did was bring forward what I was going to say by twenty-four months. It was very easy to do.

Mr Carswell leaves the Commons with few regrets.

It's a huge privilege and an enormous honour being an MP and I absolutely loved serving Clacton and I absolutely adore doing the things I do in the constituency and I'm not just saying that, I genuinely do. But I never particularly liked the House of Commons life. I was there for a purpose [to campaign to leave the European Union], and once that purpose was done [it was time to leave].

There are some wonderful people in the Commons, but there are an awful lot of people who have been there for thirty-something years and I'm not sure they know what they're doing there. I'm not sure anyone knows. It becomes a way of life.

I will really miss the library there, an amazing facility; you can order any book you want, brilliant stuff. There are some lovely people on both the sides of the Chamber who are wonderful [but] I don't really want to be doing in my late forties what I was doing in my early thirties. I have got a million-and-one interests that have got nothing whatsoever to do with politics.

Soon after I became an MP, Robin Cook, who was a great statesman and a highly respected Labour frontbencher, died of a heart attack. And it had quite a profound effect on me because I suddenly realised that all of us are just passing through.

We might congregate in the tea rooms or the corridors, but the Commons doesn't belong to any of us. Make of it what you will, do what you want while you're there, but it's not ours. If we are lucky we have a leasehold on it for five years. No one gets the freehold.

Mr Carswell looks back on his time in the Commons with a sense of pride, and completeness. He says:

It's a huge honour, being able to call myself a Member of Parliament for Clacton. I can't think of a single higher honour. You hear of people being given knighthoods and being made peers, you hear of people getting all sorts of things, [but] actually to call yourself a Member of Parliament for Clacton is the highest privilege I could possibly have.

Clacton has been very good to me. I have never lost an election there. I just think that I did my best.

CV

Born in Uganda, educated in Uganda and England. Worked in investment management and Conservative Party Policy Unit.

2001 unsuccessfully contests Sedgefield.
2005 elected MP for Harwich.
2009 tables bill calling for referendum on British

membership of the European Union; leads campaign to force Speaker Michael Martin from office.

2010   elected MP for Clacton.

2014   defects to UK Independence Party, re-elected MP for Clacton.

2016   campaigns for Leave during EU referendum.

2017   leaves UK Independence Party, sits as an Independent, stands down from Parliament.

Married to Clementine, one daughter.

SIR EDWARD GARNIER

Sir Edward Garnier, 64, was Conservative MP for Harborough 1992–2017.

How did you end up in Parliament?

'I joined in 1976 the [barristers'] chambers I am now in, and Leon Britton was a member of those chambers, and by then was already a Member of Parliament. I used to go and chat to him. He said: "Why don't you go and do something rather than just talk about it?" And that encouraged me.'

How did you feel on first becoming an MP?

'It was very exciting. The first thing I remember was queueing up to take the oath, and Michael Bates, who is now in the Lords, was just behind me in the queue. Somebody said: "He's a lot younger than you and will last a lot longer, let him go in front of you, and then there is a chance he might become Father of the House." He did [go in front], although he lost his seat after.'

Best of times:

'Going into office [as Solicitor General in 2010] was great after twelve, thirteen years in opposition. No matter how important you think you are as shadow Secretary of State for Drawing Pins, you can't actually achieve anything. You can make speeches which nobody reports, make proposals which nobody takes up, but in our system you need to be in government to get things done. And there I was at last, after all those years, in government. Great fun.'

Worst of times:

'Not being kept on the front bench by Iain Duncan Smith. Although he was a friend, who had come in at the same time as me, he was not someone I thought was up to the job of being Leader of the Opposition.'

Why are you leaving?

'The old cliché is it's better to go when people are asking you, "Why are you leaving?" than staying on and people saying, "Why are you still here?" I'll be sixty-five in October this year, my faculties still just about function, and I thought, "Well, I may as well just go."'

What are your thoughts for future MPs?

'It's an incredible privilege to be one of the 650 Members of Parliament, so do enjoy it. And whilst I would urge them to take the job extremely seriously, every now and then I think they ought to just sit back and puncture their own balloon.'

Will you have any regrets about leaving the Commons? And what are you going to do next?

'I feel a slight sense of liberation that I won't have to deal with the 250 emails I used to get every day. I won't have to deal with the eccentricities of some of the more eccentric constituents. But I will miss, quite severely, the friends that I have made in Parliament. I will miss the good friends I made within the constituency, within the Conservative Association.

Continue at the bar. Go on holiday.'

SIR EDWARD GARNIER: THE FULL STORY

Sir Edward Garnier was born in Germany, where his father was a Colonel in the British Army. He says:

My father was an army officer and when he retired he went back to my uncle's farm and became his land agent, so politics was not at the forefront of his life, except as a recipient of it, in the sense that he was an army officer. My mother was clearly interested in day-to-day events that were going on, but neither of them was intensely political. But both my mother's family and my father's family have, this sounds awful, over the centuries been involved in politics. The first member of my mother's family to get into Parliament was in 1546; it was Henry VIII's last parliament. My father's family didn't get in until after the Revocation of the Edict of Nantes [which withdrew religious freedom for Protestants in France] in about 1689. They soon got into political life. Broadly from the late eighteenth, early nineteenth centuries they were starting to take an active role in elected politics rather than just being people on the boundaries. My wife's family have similarly been in politics since the turn of the sixteenth, seventeenth centuries, so it's always been there in the background, but it wasn't a force, like some sort of magnetic field, it was just sort of there. When I did it, nobody was terribly surprised, although not very enamoured of my doing it.

From the outset, Sir Edward was always clear where his political sympathies lay. 'I was never tempted as a schoolboy or as an undergraduate or someone in my twenties to join any other party than the Conservatives,' he says.

On leaving Oxford, Sir Edward entered the law. He didn't seriously turn his mind to politics until the mid-1970s, by which time his career as a barrister was well established. 'I suppose there is a connection between the sort of work a barrister does and the sort of work a Member of Parliament does: speaking on others' behalf, dealing with the law, getting up on one's hind feet.'

As a first step towards entering Parliament, Sir Edward became involved in politics at a local level. 'I lived in Wandsworth Borough, which was an intensely political borough, and in those days was very heavily Labour. Now Wandsworth is a byword for Conservative borough politics but in those days it was exactly the opposite.' He became branch chairman of the Wandsworth Conservative Association, and then stood for the borough council.

By now determined to enter the House of Commons, he set his sights on Norfolk, the county where he had grown up, and got to the final rounds in several selections. In one, North West Norfolk, he narrowly lost out to his friend Henry Bellingham. 'He and I used to ring each other up, we had known each other since childhood, and say: "I've got through to the next round, have you?"'

To his disappointment, he failed to be selected anywhere in time for the 1983 general election, and instead prepared to fight a 'no hoper' the next time around. He found himself in Hemsworth, West Yorkshire, a solidly Labour seat where the Conservatives were in third place. 'That taught me a lot about politics,' Sir Edward says.

The Conservative Association had probably a membership of about twenty. It had no office, no agent, no staff. It just had a lot of very hard-working, very brave volunteers, who had stuck to being Conservative throughout the miners' strike in the early '80s, and a number of them at considerable personal risk. My chairman, a wonderful woman, and her husband, kept horses under rules and they had their hay barn burnt down because they were seen as collaborators with the Thatcher government.

There was one woman, who I'm still in touch with now, whose job it was to go out at night to stick up posters for the Conservative Party. It was like being a member of the French resistance, she used to come home at dawn and she used to be physically sick, [she was] so terrified of what would have happened if she had been caught. Her husband was a coalminer, and so she was incredibly brave.

That was a great learning experience and it taught me that there are some people who are Conservatives on purpose rather just by upbringing, and I really admired that, I thought it was superb. It was an amazing place to cut my teeth as a parliamentary candidate.

On election night 1987, and despite the fact that the sitting Labour MP enjoyed a 14,000 majority, Sir Edward even had hopes of entering the Commons. 'It's funny how elections get to you, he says. 'I went to bed on election night thinking I might just pull this one off. We came second as opposed to third, which was where we had been before.'

Undeterred, Sir Edward set about trying again. 'The next thing I did was apply for safe seats,' he says. 'I wanted a seat either in Norfolk, where I grew up, or in Leicestershire, where my wife up grew up. And very luckily, in January 1990, I was selected for Harborough. So that was wonderful.'

Harborough, in south-east Leicestershire, was held by the Conservatives with a majority of nearly 20,000, so, barring a disaster, Sir Edward could now be confident of becoming an MP. 'I knew I was going to be elected as the Member of Parliament, but I was also convinced that we were going to go into opposition,' he says.

This was John Major's election, having taken over as Prime Minister eighteen months earlier. It was very clear to me that we were going to lose – and then we won.

Election night didn't exist. In those days in Harborough, the council didn't want to pay overtime, so they carried out the count during the morning. Harborough and the Outer Hebrides were the only two seats that hadn't declared by dawn on 9 April 1992. I wasn't declared the winner until about one or two o'clock on Friday afternoon.

When he finally arrived in the Commons, Sir Edward set

about getting used to his new life, and becoming acquainted with his colleagues.

I wasn't a policy wonk and I didn't belong to the Oxford University Conservative Association [or] the Oxford Union. I didn't belong to any of the gatherings of young politicians, except for my work in Wandsworth. So I didn't know a huge number of other candidates, although I was part of a group called the 'Standard Bearers'. We were a group of rather self-regarding young men, although I was nearly forty, who largely assumed we would be in the Cabinet the Wednesday after the election. We wrote a moderately interesting pamphlet called 'Bearing the Standard.'

I shared a room with three others ... and we were rather like schoolboys or undergraduates sharing a room. It enabled us to get used to this extraordinary new existence without being lonely. There was a lot of schoolboy teasing. *The House* magazine [Parliament's own publication] did one of those awful surveys – what are your ambitions – and Charles Hendry made the mistake of saying that his ambition was to be my ministerial driver, an ambition which he singularly failed to achieve. We had fun, and we got on with the serious business of representing our constituents.

So I had a very lucky introduction and in my first few months I had a very happy time.

Despite John Major's unexpected victory, the Commons Sir Edward arrived in was going through a turbulent time, as Eurosceptic rebels in the Conservative Party attempted to thwart the passage of the Maastricht Treaty, leading to knife-edge votes and all-night sittings.

'I made my maiden speech in the Maastricht committee stage on the floor of the House, about 12.30, one o'clock in the morning,' he says.

Douglas Hurd, the Foreign Secretary, came in to listen, which was very kind of him. He wrote me a very nice letter that evening.

My wife rang up the Members' Lobby, just outside the Chamber, and spoke to one of the doorkeepers, and said: 'Where is my husband?' 'Well, he's just made a speech.' 'When do you expect him to finish?' 'Probably at about nine o'clock in the morning.' There was a lot of that during Maastricht. We used to sit late, sometimes all night. On one or two occasions the thing went beyond nine or ten o'clock so you lost the next day's business. It meant for me going home at dawn, having had a shower, changing, and then going into chambers to earn a living. So they were longer days, but because it was new, it was exhilarating. It was great fun.

At the start of his time in Parliament, Sir Edward had been

determined not to be pigeon-holed as a lawyer. He took a keen interest in foreign affairs, and became secretary of the Conservative Backbench Foreign Affairs Committee, before taking his first step on the ministerial ladder as a parliamentary private secretary in the Foreign Office. But due to a combination of circumstance and a certain amount of typecasting by the leadership, he found he kept being drawn back to his roots.

'I came into Parliament to some extent wanting to get away from the law,' he says.

There I was at the age of thirty-nine and a half coming into Parliament, and could clearly see myself as the next Home Secretary, or next Foreign Secretary, next something else that would suit my suitably high opinion of myself.

My law has been both an advantage and something I didn't want to be an anchor tying me down to the job of a shadow law officer or a law officer, albeit as I got into Parliament over the years, and then into the government, even though it wasn't necessarily what I wanted to do when I got there, [I began to feel that] if I had a strength I might as well use it.

There is plenty that I have enjoyed about combining the law and politics. Both [for their own sake], and also because it has enabled me, I think, to be a better informed Member of Parliament about an awful lot of what government and Parliament does.

After the 1997 general election, Sir Edward was appointed by the new leader, William Hague, to what would become a series of posts related to the law.

I was obviously hoping that William Hague would put me on the front bench at some level, albeit that I had been a Ken Clarke supporter in that [leadership] election. He made me shadow spokesman for the Lord Chancellor's department. He said: 'I'm afraid I'm keeping you in the law,' as if it were a terrible thing to be boxed in to be something to do with the law. Well, I was on the front bench, that wasn't bad. It wasn't the sexiest political job in the world, but there were plenty of colleagues who weren't on the front bench at all.

Sir Edward entered the 2001 general election as shadow Attorney General, but two disappointments followed. Having again backed the veteran Europhile Kenneth Clarke in the contest which came in the wake of Mr Hague's resignation, following the party's second loss to New Labour, he was unimpressed by the choice of Iain Duncan Smith as leader. The latter then dismissed him from the front bench – in a highly public manner.

I was sitting in my room and I had happened by chance to have bought the *Daily Telegraph* to read on the Tube that morning, and it said in the *Daily Telegraph* that Edward Garnier was to be replaced as shadow Attorney General by Bill Cash. Well, that was quite funny. Later that afternoon, about five o'clock, I was sitting at my desk in Chambers, and Owen Paterson, who was again a friend of mine but was Duncan Smith's PPS, rang me up and said: 'I've got the leader on the line.' I said: 'Well, put the leader on then.'

Iain came on and was coughing and spluttering and said: 'I'm just calling to let you know that I'm not keeping you on as shadow Attorney General.' I said: 'Yeah, I know that, I read it in this morning's *Telegraph*.' Whereupon he got in a frightful embarrassment. And I said: 'For goodness sake, don't worry about it. These things happen and, anyway, you're entitled to have your little gang around you rather than anyone else's.' It was amusing, but also nobody likes getting the sack, even in the esteemed columns of the *Daily Telegraph*.

With the election of David Cameron as leader in 2005, Sir Edward returned to frontline politics, first as a shadow Home Affairs minister, then shadow Justice, with responsibility for prisons, a role he relished.

I wrote a paper called 'Prisons with a Purpose', and I have always since then taken an acute interest in prisons policy and prisons reform. I am a patron of a charity called Unlock, and I'm a trustee of the Prison Reform Trust, so I've maintained my interest in that aspect of public policy.

With the 2010 election approaching, Sir Edward was promoted to the shadow Cabinet, as shadow Attorney General, his second spell in the job, and he had every expectation of becoming the real thing if the Conservatives were victorious. Instead, with the emergence of the Tory–Liberal Democrat coalition, things became a little messy.

For the formation of the coalition everybody got shunted sideways or downwards, so I got shunted downwards from Attorney to Solicitor [General] and [Dominic] Grieve got shunted sideways from Justice Secretary [to Attorney General].

So it was a mixture of disappointment and delight when I was appointed Solicitor General, but it was a job I did enjoy and it taught me not to get frustrated. Politics is such an extraordinary business, you can be up one minute and down the next and up again whenever. I had always thought of politics to some extent as a form of organised disappointment.

Despite being given the lesser of the law officer roles, Sir Edward found this time in government the most enjoyable experience of his career in Parliament. He learned to appreciate the constitutional significance of a role which, while somewhat niche, was nonetheless crucial to the smooth operation of government. 'The great thing about being a law officer is that only the law officers understand what they are for,' he says.

If you ask the average Member of Parliament what does the Attorney General do or what does the Solicitor General do … by and large they didn't know that they supervise the prosecuting authorities, protect the national interest, and appear in court in cases in Strasbourg and in Luxembourg; the High Court, the Court of Appeal, and the Supreme Court here.

It's that funny hybrid between being a political minister bound by collective responsibility, but also something separate, something apolitical, something outside the normal run and bustle of politics.

It's both a metaphor and geographically true. The law officers have their offices within the House of Commons, just off Central Lobby, so away from all the other political ministers' offices. They were there to enable them to run up the stairs to the judicial committee to argue cases in front of the old House of Lords. But it was also so they could not be tainted by, or influenced by, or interfered with by, the Prime Minister or political ministers popping into their room and saying: 'Don't you think we ought to prosecute this bloke?' It's a funny job, it was hard work, but I enjoyed it.

Although the law officers rarely get an opportunity to introduce legislation, as Solicitor General Sir Edward was able to bring in one measure, a procedure called a 'Deferred Prosecution Agreement', which allows corporations to delay prosecution while they abide by certain conditions. Since their introduction, he himself in his other job as a barrister has used these Agreements twice on behalf of the Serious Fraud Office.

The last one was Rolls Royce, which I did in January of this year, where the Serious Fraud Office agreed with Rolls Royce that it should pay over half a billion pounds in penalties for corruption between 1989 and 2012. That was one of my great highs, as a non-political minister, getting a bit of policy in.

To his disappointment, in 2012, for reasons he was never entirely clear about, Sir Edward was returned to the back benches by David Cameron.

A lot of people on the Conservative benches who had been shadow ministers had a reasonable expectation that they would be translated from being shadow minister to take up a substantive role in government, and they weren't.

I think David Cameron thought, 'Well, I had better give more people a go at being in office.'

I'm reasonably sure that he thought that Edward Garnier wasn't the sort of chap who was going to burst into tears and make a fuss. And he was right in that. When I went into his room in the House of Commons, and he said: 'I'm going to move you on,' he said: 'You don't seem to be getting into a frightful lather about this.' I said: 'What's the point?' It was harder [than being sacked by Iain Duncan Smith] in a sense because I was being removed from a real office rather than a shadow office. I thought I was doing a very good job, of course I did, as Solicitor General.

Although he enjoyed the last five years as a backbencher, Sir Edward was not tempted to remain in the Commons once Theresa May called an election. He says.

I was always intending to leave in 2020, by which time I would have done twenty-eight years. I would have been over sixty-seven and I thought that was enough. When Theresa May, at short notice – I certainly didn't know she was going to do it – called this election, I then had to work out: do I want to go on until I'm just short of seventy, or do I go now when I don't have a Zimmer frame, I don't dribble and I'm young enough and fit enough to do other things as well as carrying on my practice at the bar? I decided it was better to go now.

Sir Edward will continue to live in Harborough, and will continue to work as a barrister. He says: 'Because my wife comes from [Leicestershire], we are staying there. It's where we brought the children up. They're all adults now, and I've got a grandchild, and my grandchild is the same age as my youngest son was when I first became elected.'

While he has come full circle in his private life, Sir Edward also sees some symmetry to his political career. 'I came in on Maastricht and I'm going out on Brexit,' he says. 'It's not a bad thing to be a Member of Parliament. I can go to my grave saying "Twenty-five years as a Member of Parliament isn't too bad an epitaph."'

CV

Born in Germany, raised in Norfolk, called to the Bar 1973.

1987 unsuccessfully contests Hemsworth.
1992 elected MP for Harborough.
1994 appointed PPS to Alastair Goodlad and David Davis at Foreign Office.
1996 appointed PPS to Nicholas Lyell, the Attorney General.

1997   appointed PPS to Roger Freeman, Chancellor of the Duchy of Lancashire; appointed shadow spokesman on the Lord Chancellor's Department.

1999   appointed shadow Attorney General.

2001   sacked from front bench.

2005   appointed shadow Home Affairs minister.

2007   appointed shadow Justice minister.

2009   appointed shadow Attorney General.

2010   appointed Solicitor General.

2012   sacked from Cabinet, knighted.

2015   appointed to Privy Council.

2017   stands down from Parliament.

Married to Anna, three children.

IAIN WRIGHT

Iain Wright, 45, was Labour MP for Hartlepool 2004–17.

How did you end up in Parliament?

'Peter Mandelson resigned. So my lottery ticket came up then. I was in exactly the right place at the right time to represent my own seat.'

How did you feel on first becoming an MP?

'It felt a bit like how it must feel if you are the Rolling Stones and have been on tour for two years, and have been told what to do; so Tuesday you will be doing this, Wednesday you will be doing that. And then the tour stops, and it is, well now, actually I have to get on with the job.'

Best of times:

'Making the speech at St Martin in the Fields announcing our rough sleeping strategy, that was my best day. [I] really pushed that, pledging that we were going to completely eradicate rough sleeping on the streets of Britain by 2012. I got Gordon [Brown] interested, this was going to be a real social policy.'

Worst of times:

'I hadn't been an MP very long, and the Boxing Day tsunami [happened]. Somebody from the constituency had lost somebody. I had written a note to them saying, and I remember those phrases: "I just wanted to write to say I'm really sorry, and if there is anything I can do just let me know." I did it with the best of intentions, it wasn't going to go to the press or anything like that, and they wrote back and they just went: "How dare you?" And then they sent it to the local paper. It really upset me. I tried to do the right thing and I got slated for it. And it was grief, I understand that, but all I was doing was trying to help.'

Why are you leaving?

'I want to do different things. I was forty-five last month and in terms of the election being called now, it's probably a lot easier to embark on something new at forty-five than, say, at forty-eight. I like the idea of doing different chapters.'

What are your thoughts for future MPs?

'Enjoy it, it's an enormous privilege. And never lose sight of why you are going into it. Think about the honour. And think about public service.'

Do you have any regrets about leaving the Commons? And what are you going to do next?

'You always leave with unfinished business, but I suppose, to get philosophical, you can't always do everything you want to do in life, can you? I have been very fortunate that virtually as soon as I announced I was going to leave I've been offered another job. It's everything I love, really. If I boil down what I've tried to do in politics; I want to champion the North East, because it's the region I love, I want to champion industry. So it's being chief executive of a body of science, chemical and pharmaceutical firms that do that. It's called NEPIC – North East Process Industry Cluster. It's a great job.'

IAIN WRIGHT: THE FULL STORY

Politics was not discussed much at home when Iain Wright was growing up in Hartlepool in County Durham, but, he says, it was in the air. 'I didn't come from a political family,' he says.

There is a story in the family that there was a Tory elected in Hartlepool at some point and my grandmother, my dad's mother, went down at the count and she shouted at him. I don't think that's true. [The family was] not political at all [but] growing up in the 1980s in the North East, you just saw factory after factory close. It was difficult not to be political. There was just that general sense of decay, the general sense of, well, the government doesn't seem to be helping round here very much, and why does it have to be like this? So I have always been interested in politics in that regard.

There was, however, one member of the family who took more of an interest in politics: Mr Wright's grandfather, who helped to raise him during his early childhood and engaged in long discussions about socialism. 'A big influence on my life was my granddad,' he says.

He had been a steelworker and then he got ill. He used to do things with motorbikes and then had a big motorbike accident and couldn't work and my Mam and my Nana both worked, so essentially my life was at my granddad's knee. He taught me everything. He taught me about The Beatles, and he taught me about socialism and he taught me about politics, so I'm shaped a lot by that. He died when I was nine. I would have loved some of the fights that we would have had about politics.

By the time he was in his teens, Mr Wright had joined his local Labour Party. He 'did bits and bobs in the local party', then became a councillor when he was still in his twenties and working as a chartered accountant. His path to the Commons was exceptionally smooth. Hartlepool had been represented since 1992 by Peter Mandelson, one of the architects of New Labour and a divisive figure both locally and on the national stage. When, in 2004, Mr Mandelson resigned his seat to become a European Commissioner, triggering a by-election, the field was open for Mr Wright to succeed him. 'Luck plays a part in these things,' he says.

> I was the treasurer of the local party and I had thought about [becoming an MP but] I hadn't really contemplated a seat other than Hartlepool. I wouldn't probably have done it outside the North East. I was on the MPs' selection panel, but the lottery ticket came up then; right place right time, and, if I am honest, the right sort of person. Peter was a national figure, and I think they wanted someone very local at the time; grounded.

Hartlepool was a safe Labour seat, but there was a certain amount of anger locally at Mr Mandelson's departure, and Mr Wright faced a serious threat from the Liberal Democrats. From the moment of his selection he was confident he would end up in the House of Commons, however. 'I never doubted it,' he says.

> That might sound arrogant, but it's not. I think it's just that I knew my town, and it was a great by-election team. It was a long campaign, about ten weeks, but there were no doubts about it. I was just confident that we would be able to do it.

Mr Wright found the experience of campaigning in the glare of national attention which most by-elections attract a mixed experience. 'In many respects it's really horrible,' he says.

> Because I actually don't like attention very much. I know I've chosen the wrong profession completely to [be like] that in terms of trying to be quite private [given] the nature of the by-election. My wife was pregnant at the time, so it was a case of wanting to photograph her, photograph the bump, everybody got involved in the family in photos. It was a bit strange. Being centre of attention was an odd thing; bizarre. It was a long campaign.

On election night, 23 July 2004, Mr Wright learned he had squeaked home with a majority of just over 2,000. Amid the chaos of the count, his grandfather was high in his thoughts.

I got a lot of stick for this at the time, which I felt was grossly unfair, but I thanked him in my speech, just saying: 'It was thanks to you,' or something like that. My best mate who lives in London came up for the count, because I wanted him there as well. The sound system wasn't very good, so I couldn't really hear myself. And then at the count the Fathers4Justice [fathers' rights campaigners] poured purple powder over the Lib Dem candidate, so it was all a bit nasty and a bit surreal as well. By-elections are by-elections, and if you think about it, one of the remarkable things is that we won it. Seven years into a Labour government, there wasn't a death or anything, Peter had chosen to go and do something else. Talk about formidable election machines, the Lib Dems were on fire at that point, but, yeah, we had a great team, I was really fortunate, and pushed it over the line.

Arriving in the House of Commons, Mr Wright found it difficult to adjust from life on the campaign trail to the more sedate pace of Parliament. But he found plenty of colleagues willing to help him settle in. 'I knew a few people,' he says.

Certainly being active in the North East Labour Party meant I knew people, and people had come up [to Hartlepool]. One of the things about a by-election is people have seen you. But it's also interesting because you are left on your own. The whole support system is then dropped, which is slightly odd.

I have read biographies where the likes of Roy Jenkins and Denis Healey were saying, I work in the library or did my correspondence sat on a radiator for six months. It wasn't like that at all [for me]. I turned up on the Monday and I had an office. In that regard it was very slick.

In terms of the personal support, the 2001 intake, the likes of Andy Burnham, Chris Bryant, Kevin Brennan, Tom Watson, Kevan Jones, who had actually been my by-election support person, just took me as their own. So I was always classed as the 2001 intake which was really kind. I didn't feel intimidated, actually; I wanted to do stuff, I wanted to represent my constituents. I remember speaking to a Serjeant-at-Arms officer and he was saying, 'You've been here a couple of weeks, Mr Wright, how are you finding it?' I said: 'Well it's a bit odd isn't it?' And he was going: 'Mr Wright, we've been doing this for 800 years, I think we've got it right now.' Which I thought was great.

I remember making my maiden speech, a really vivid recollection, and looking up at the clock and going: 'I quite enjoy this.' I had obviously been quite nervous beforehand, but I was thinking, 'I quite enjoy this.' I've always been quite nervous speaking in the chamber because I have always found it really important. But I enjoyed it as well.

With Tony Blair's second term in office drawing to a close, Mr Wright was conscious throughout his first months in Parliament that he would be forced to fight an election again before too long. 'I was basically in campaign mode the whole time,' he says.

In many respects it was a very long eight or nine months, learning the job, trying to be a responsive MP, and still thinking about [the fact that] there's going to be an election in eight or nine months. I was always interested in economic and financial matters so I tended to focus on that. Coming from where I came from, and I am a professional chartered accountant, those were the things that interested me. You can solve a lot of society's problems by solving the economic challenges. So I have always gone in that direction. And of course, three weeks after becoming an MP, my wife gives birth to our son as well.

Mr Wright admits he was ambitious, so he was pleased when, after the 2005 general election in which he increased his majority to nearly 7,500, he took the first step on the ministerial ladder as a parliamentary private secretary. 'I wanted to be a minister, I wanted to change things,' he says.

I was a PPS immediately after the 2005 election to Rosie [Winterton]. She was in the Department of Health. I have never worked so hard in my life. She is such a hard taskmaster. And also I have never laughed so much in my life. She was brilliant, because she basically said: 'You just do what you want and be at every single meeting in the department.' So in terms of how to be a minister and how to operate in Whitehall, she was absolutely fantastic.

From his first days in Westminster, Mr Wright was associated with supporters of Gordon Brown. When, in September 2006, a group of PPSs loyal to Mr Brown resigned in a bid to put pressure on Tony Blair to make way for him, Mr Wright joined in. He says that although he had enjoyed his time with Ms Winterton, the attempted coup against Mr Blair was not the only reason he wanted to step down, with a number of family crises and concerns in his constituency about the closure of a hospital also playing a role. 'That was a strange year actually. My Nana died, eight days later my son had a stroke, and then there was a local thing about a hospital and it was all linked in with that,' he says.

From a local point of view there was concern about the local hospital and I wasn't getting the reassurances I needed. And it was a case of, I'm a PPS in the Department of Health, this is absolutely ridiculous, I'm going to have to go. And linked in with this was the whole PPS thing in terms of the Tony thing. So it all coincided.

When Mr Brown did finally become Prime Minister, in the summer of 2007, Mr Wright was rewarded with a fully-fledged ministerial post, first in the Department for Communities and later the Department for Children, Schools and Families. What followed was his most fulfilling time in Parliament when, as a minister, he found himself able to have a genuine impact on people's lives.

'I got into government when Gordon took over,' he says.

You can change things in government, and that's the whole point I think. Being a PPS, being a junior minister, in many respects you are shaped by what the Secretary of State and Prime Minister want to do. I was very lucky because I had two great senior ministers, Yvette Cooper and Ed Balls, who basically said, 'What do you want to do? What element of the brief do you want?' Which was great.

I had two briefs: I had housing and planning [at the Communities Department], and in Children Schools and Families I had curriculum reform, skills and apprenticeships. So they were fantastic, they were real, real, real jobs. It was great stuff to be able to get your teeth into.

Some of the regeneration stuff, the old Northern towns,

the old housing stock, pulling down the old two-up, two-downs, and putting in new modern housing, I had responsibility for that, under the Housing Market Renewal programme. Writing [a] check for £1 billion to do the Housing Market Renewal … to change things in northern towns and cities, that was pretty good. The housing market was really important, just to provide that catalyst for good, decent housing in northern areas. The best part for me [about those policies was] I think it shows what a Labour government can do.

During his three years as a minister, Mr Wright grew accustomed to the Commons Chamber, and came to love answering questions on behalf of his department.

I really enjoyed being at the despatch box because it was exhilarating, terrifying, and you are so, so alone. You are very conscious that actually you are saying the policy of Her Majesty's government, and, if you fuck it up, that's really bad. So it's all those different emotions. I used to love it.

As the 2010 general election approached, Mr Wright was still hoping that Gordon Brown might remain as Prime Minister – and that his life as a minister could continue. He says:

In 2010, going round the streets and knocking on doors and people beeping their car horns and thanking you and giving you the thumbs up, I remember going home and saying to Tiff, my wife, 'Do you know, I think we could get a Labour government here.' And she said: 'Don't be so bloody stupid, of course not.'

With the formation of the coalition government, Mr Wright found himself on the opposition benches, an experience he describes as disconcerting at the outset and then increasingly depressing. He says: 'My wife is the most politically astute person I know, and she went: "You'll hate it, you'll really, really hate it." I said, "I won't, I'll blame the Tories for everything."'

But he did hate it.

You walk into the chamber and instead of going right you go left. That hit me. That took me months to get used to, walking in and going 'shit!' I think for a good six months it really affected me.

I was [shadow] Education minister, and one of the first bills [of the coalition was] the Academies Bill. Trying to think about how to respond and then seeing your private office passing notes to the minister was like seeing an ex-girlfriend of yours snogging someone else. It was really strange. I used to see them more often than I saw my family, and then you see them passing notes to someone else. It's really odd.

It was some consolation that in his last term in office, from 2015, Mr Wright was elected to the role of chairman of the Commons Business, Skills and Innovation Committee, where he proved a formidable inquisitor of, among others, Sir Philip Green, the disgraced businessman, over the collapse of BHS, and Mike Ashley, the owner of the troubled Sports Direct firm, which was accused of ill-treating workers and the use of immoral, if not illegal, practices such as zero-hours contracts.

Mr Wright says of his role in the high profile inquiries:

It's amazing, how many people [were aware of them]. Just a few days ago I was shopping in a supermarket and someone wanted to say: 'I really enjoyed what you did with Philip Green and Mike Ashley.'

The chairmanship of the select committee was a great way of trying to get some stuff done. One of the things I'm really proud of [are] the reports we did on industrial strategy and corporate governance. They didn't get the drama and the high-profile like Philip Green and Mike Ashley, but they are really good, well researched, extraordinarily perceptive pieces of work. But we are not going to implement them. We are sort of commentating. And that's the frustrating thing.

By the time he took on the chairmanship of the select committee, Mr Wright had already decided he would like to try his hand at something new following the end of the parliament. He speaks of John Freeman, the great Labour MP, diplomat and broadcaster, as an example of a public figure who had a number of different careers. He found life in opposition dispiriting, and had little expectation that under new leader Jeremy Corbyn, Labour would be in power any time soon. Nor did his political views chime with those of the leadership.

'The personal collides with the political,' he says of his decision to stand down.

I wasn't going to do 2020. I had said to my wife [at the 2015 general election], 'One more go, I will do one more.' There is an importance to opposition which is absolutely invaluable, but I want to change things, and it's a case of, is being an opposition MP the best way to try and change things?

It seemed that we were [going to be] out [of office] for a significant period of time. [The Corbyn view is] not an agenda that I necessarily agree with. I don't want to be critical, I haven't said anything publicly, and one of the reasons is that when the circus leaves, the circus leaves. There are good colleagues [still in Parliament], and the idea of a former colleague saying: 'This is all crap,' I think would make their job just a little bit harder. I didn't want to do that.

Mr Wright has a few regrets about leaving the Commons with unfinished business.

> The select committee had a great report starting about the future world of work, how we are going to cope with the rise of automation and all of that, and it's a shame that we haven't done that. So, yeah, there will be some pangs, but I think it's a case of you don't look back. You do other things.

For a somewhat shy man, stepping out of the limelight will come as a relief, particularly given what he sees as a toxic drift towards a more hostile view of politics and politicians among the public. 'What I won't miss is the notion that everything I do should be seen as a negative thing,' he says.

> Everything that MPs do, they're in it for themselves, all of that. Because, in the main, regardless of party, that's not true. It got worse I think after 2010, I noticed the change. I'm not suggesting that people used to doff their caps, there was nothing like that, they were no more deferential and nor should they have been. But the idea of where you are coming from, are you coming from a really cynical jaded point of view, or are you going, well, actually, yeah, I'm going to scrutinise you, and I'm going to question you, that changed a lot. And it's getting progressively worse and Twitter and social media makes it worse. It's like me and

you holding a megaphone and just shouting at each other and not listening. Now, I'm not suggesting that there was a golden age where people thought, well I will read the manifestos and I'll come down on what I think is best for the country. But there is [now] an inherent anger, and an unwillingness to engage with an opposing point of view, the black and white elements, you're either for or against, [which] really pisses me off. Because, actually, life is not like that. There is a bit of a grey.

In the main, however, Mr Wright looks back on his time in Parliament with pride. 'I loved it, I just loved the place, I really loved it,' he says.

You don't take it for granted, you think, I've only got a job for four or five years – or two years, as it turns out. I'm pleased with what I've achieved. There was some good stuff as minister. We had a great select committee, a great team, fantastic clerks and we did some really, really good stuff. There was always the possibility of doing a bit more, but there was also the possibility of going off and doing something related but slightly different and that's what I want to do. I think life is about doing different things. Maybe [it's] attention deficit, I don't know, but [I have] the notion of: I've done that, I'm going to go and do something else now.

CV

Born and raised in Hartlepool, chartered accountant.

2004   elected MP for Hartlepool.

2005   becomes PPS to Rosie Winterton at Department of Health.

2006   resigns from government.

2007   becomes Communities minister.

2009   becomes Minister for Children, Schools and Families.

2010   becomes shadow Minister for Children, Schools and Families, becomes shadow Education minister.

2011   becomes shadow Business minister.

2015   becomes chairman of Business, Innovation and Skills Committee.

2017   stands down from Parliament.

Married to Tiffany, four children.

SIR ERIC PICKLES

Sir Eric Pickles, 65, was Conservative MP for Brentwood & Ongar 1992–2017.

How did you end up in Parliament?

'I was looking aimlessly out of a window wondering what I should do and suddenly at my right elbow somebody took me in a vice-like grip that was very solid and if I'm honest rather painful. And there was Margaret Thatcher. She said: "Come with me," and walked me across to the chap who was running the candidates. She said: "This is Mr Pickles. Mr Pickles would like to be a Member of Parliament and I would very much like Mr Pickles to be a Member of Parliament."'

How did you feel on first becoming an MP?

'I felt at ease at the Commons pretty much straight away.

I was very comfortable. It was such a great privilege to represent a constituency.'

Best of times:
'I can narrow down exactly the moment I was the happiest, which was the first oral questions of Communities and Local Government. I spent several days getting ready for it. This was the first time, I had to answer pretty carefully. I had this witty little thing to say when I got to the despatch box.

Speaker called my name, I stood up. I touched the side of the despatch box, I touched the brass corner pieces, and this enormous wave, this tsunami of ginormous proportions of happiness, hit me. I thought: "This is just the coolest thing, it's unbelievable. I'm so happy." And then I looked up, and the opposition are looking at me, I looked at the Speaker and he's smiling at me, and I thought: "I think you had better say something."'

Worst of times:
'We won '92 unexpectedly; there were lots of things facing this country, and we just went into self-destruct mode. I am a happy chappy. Nothing much upsets me. But I found it absolutely hideous. Dreadful.

There were times when I couldn't abide being in the

lobbies with people really enjoying defeating John Major on Maastricht.'

Why are you leaving?

'I have done twenty-five years, and I have seen many a Member stay on too long to do just one more parliament [and] become a bed blocker. It would have been so easy to have stayed on, do things I like, but I think parliamentary institutions require renewal.'

What are your thoughts for future MPs?

'You've got to decide where you stand. You've got to decide what's important to you. Politics is always about deals, politics is always about making that compromise, but don't allow yourself to get lost in that. It will end. Enjoy it.'

Will you any have regrets on leaving the Commons? And what are you going to do next?

'Of course I will regret it. There are times when I think: "What on earth are you doing?" But was it the right thing to do? Absolutely.

I've got a directorship in a small recycling company, and I'm quite enjoying the rigours of commercial reality. They're nice people, I rather like them, and it's nice to be connected to reality.'

SIR ERIC PICKLES: THE FULL STORY

Sir Eric Pickles was born in 1952 in Keighley, West York-shire, and grew up helping his father in his grocers' shop. The idea of voting Conservative was so alien to his parents they would later find it 'hilarious' that he became a Tory. 'I didn't have a political family,' he says.

> My family were Labour voters. My great-grandfather was associated with the founding of the Independent Labour Party in Yorkshire. If anything I probably inclined towards Communism. For my fifteenth birthday my parents, on my request, got me [Leon] Trotsky's *History of the Russian Revolution*, which I read cover to cover.

Had it not been for a seminal world event when he was sixteen, Sir Eric may have remained on the left. But when Soviet tanks rolled into Czechoslovakia in August 1968, bringing an end to the Prague Spring, he turned his back on left-wing politics for good. 'When the Russians invad-ed, I was so utterly hacked off I thought: "What is the most outrageous thing I could do? I'll join the Conserva-tive Party as a protest." I stayed, for reasons of which I'm not entirely sure, and eventually, over a period of time, became a Conservative.'

Sir Eric quickly felt at home in the local Tory Party,

finding it a benevolent force locally. 'It was a time of radical conservatism,' he says.

> You made friends, there was just something in the place. The chairman was a mill owner, the people who were running it were greengrocers, there were people who did manual work, and one thing that I noticed was at the end of the day, if we had had a function, hands went into the Fairy Liquid regardless of how much money they had.

To begin with, his family and friends were amused by his conversion to the Conservative cause. To his regret, his mother died without seeing him take his first steps towards becoming an MP, but she had already begun to take his politics seriously by the time of her death when he was twenty-five.

'They thought it was hilarious,' he says. 'I was "Eric the Tory" for a long time. By the time both of them sadly passed away, both of them were voting Conservative, out of, I think, family loyalty.'

Within a short time of joining the party, Sir Eric became a leading light in the Young Conservatives, rising to national chairman. At the same time, he was pursuing a career in local politics – he was elected to Bradford Council in 1979, on the day Margaret Thatcher became

Prime Minister for the first time. She would come to play a crucial role in his future political career.

Although he insists he was not a Thatcherite at the outset of his 'political journey', by the time he became leader of Bradford Council, the fourth largest in the country, at the strikingly young age of thirty-six, he was fully signed up.

'I remain an unreformed, unapologetic Thatcherite,' he says. 'I had known her from the Young Conservatives, I was on the national executive of the party, she had been very kind to me in Bradford. We had taken on this Labour council and turned it into what might be described as a radical Conservative council.' In Bradford, Sir Eric was feared and applauded in equal measure, introducing an ambitious programme which included reducing the workforce by a third, privatising some services, and implementing wide-scale cuts while introducing the new community charge – known as the hated poll tax.

His endeavours in Bradford brought him to the attention of Mrs Thatcher – who decided she wanted him in Parliament, and set about getting him there. Catching sight of him at the Conservatives' annual spring conference in Scarborough, West Yorkshire, in March 1989, she marched him over to a party official and ordered him to help Sir Eric find a seat.

'It was entirely typical of Lady Thatcher,' he says.

She was that kind of person. If you needed a kick up the posterior, she would deliver it.

I was kind of wondering whether I should become an MP. I certainly talked to one or two friends who were MPs. And somebody must have blabbed. I think basically probably either [then Cabinet ministers] David Hunt or John Gummer had told her about my indecision.

So I am the accidental MP. From the period of having my elbow gripped to finding a seat that would accept me was about eighteen months.

The seat which accepted him was Brentford & Ongar in Essex, one of the safest in the country. Despite the likelihood he would become an MP, Sir Eric was not complacent ahead of his election. 'When I was selected, I thought there was more than a good chance, but I never went to a count where I didn't have two speeches prepared. Any candidate that tells you they are supremely confident of winning is a candidate that has perhaps lost touch with reality.'

He need not have worried. In the early hours of 10 April 1992, Sir Eric was elected with a majority of more than 15,000. It was, he says, an exhilarating feeling: 'Just unbelievable, just fantastic, just wonderful. I just had to ring my father. He was very proud.'

Parliament was by now a familiar place to Sir Eric, thanks to his time in the Young Conservatives, which had brought him into contact with a number of MPs and ministers.

On his first day there was confusion, however:

I arrive a few days after the election, with my wife, in my car. In those days there was virtually no security. We went into the car park – and then I was completely lost. Couldn't find my way out. A reporter managed to show me the way to get in.

We bumped into all sorts of people, future ministers, future rebels, wandering around the Houses of Parliament completely disorientated and enjoying being able to look at the paintings without being disturbed.

But thrilled as he was to be in the Commons, it was not a happy time to be a Conservative MP, as the party tore itself apart over the Maastricht Treaty, which heralded greater European unity. It was also the end of an era for the Commons, the last parliament in which late-night sittings were the norm, and the cusp of the computer age.

'The Commons was in a state of flux, a state of transition,' Sir Eric says.

I saw a little bit of what it had been like for the past two or three decades. We were beginning to see new things coming in. I've always been very tech-savvy. I remember going into the Serjeant-of-Arms office, they control these things, and asking for a modem so I could get email and go on to the web. And the chap said: 'what is a modem?' I found myself saying: 'It's like an electronic quill.'

I was the first person to get an email address in the Commons. I was one of the first people to get a computer. My secretary was in a room with a load of others, they would stand 'round to look at it.

Sir Eric says he was ambitious, eager to become a minister as soon as possible. He took his first step on the ministerial ladder within ten months, becoming a parliamentary private secretary at the Department of Industry.

Three months later, appreciating the close links he had forged in the party during his time with the Young Conservatives, the Prime Minister appointed him vice-chairman of the Conservative Party. Sir Eric would not achieve his ambition to serve in the Cabinet until David Cameron became Prime Minister during the coalition government, however. Looking back, he can afford to be relaxed about his long wait for high office, and came to relish his time within the party, which culminated with him being appointed party chairman in 2009. 'Everyone thinks they have a field marshal's baton in their rucksack.

We are a weird bunch of people, politicians, and we always have an over-inflated view of our competence,' he says.

Various promises had been made to me [during] the Major government [about a ministerial post]. But it never quite worked out. And, actually, having helped a reshuffle from the other side, it is amazing, you start off with the intention of doing something for somebody and by the time you put all the various people in place, the one you are trying to help is still left there. But I was promoted pretty quickly.

There were times when I thought I was the repository of the knowledge of the party. I have been actively involved at the top of the party since the mid-'70s, right through to a few years ago. I knew everybody, I've been there, I've had the T-shirt, I knew the history. And to tell the truth, I've always enjoyed party activities. I had been an officer of the party for just slightly over twenty years by the time I stepped down.

As somebody kindly said to me when I was party chairman, it's great to have a party chairman who actually likes the Conservative Party, which isn't always the case.

Having served in senior positions all through the long years of opposition between 1997 and 2010, Sir Eric had

no expectation of moving on from the party chairmanship following the advent of the coalition in 2010. It was
with some regret he compared himself to leading Labour
politicians who had been forced to sit out the Thatcher
years. 'I had become convinced, before David Cameron
took over, that I was going to be the Gerald Kaufman, Roy
Hattersley, of my generation. I had worked like hell, to see
other people become ministers.'

When Mr Cameron invited him to become Secretary
of State for Communities and Local Government, he was
both thrilled and confident he knew what he wanted to
do in the role. 'In those days the centre wasn't quite as all
controlling as it became by the end, and he just let me get
on with it,' he says.

Conscious that his time in office might be limited, he
was eager to get stuck in.

You have got to understand – if you're a minister, it's going
to end. So what you have got to say to yourself is: 'I am
going to do my absolute best.'

I don't want to waste the possibility. I don't want to
find myself sitting and thinking: 'If only I had done that.'
I had that very much at the forefront of my mind when
I took up office. It's not about being there, it's not about
exercising any power, it's about changing things, making a
difference. That's the important thing.

From the beginning he felt comfortable in the department even when, as it did almost straight away, something went wrong.

'I think I was a good minister because I was capable of leading a big team, and I treated the officials with respect,' he says.

I told them when they messed up to come and tell me. I wouldn't seek to blame anybody, I would try to get out of the mess.

I have to say the first time it happened they just ran away like anything. I was the first person to lose a vote in the coalition in the House of Lords. And the senior management team just hightailed it out. I was left to deal with it with a press officer and my SpAds [special advisers]. But we got through it OK.

There are some people who stand in the door and shout. I never did that. I've got a reputation for being a big bruiser; I think I treated my staff with kindness. My job was to take the rap when things went bad.

Sir Eric is proud to have served at Communities for the entire five years of the coalition. But as the 2015 election approached, he was both conscious that his time was coming to an end, and relaxed about it. Following the election, Mr Cameron told Sir Eric there would be no place for him in the first majority Conservative government since he entered Parliament in 1992.

'When good old Cameron sacked me I didn't mind much,' he says.

Some of the stuff we were doing on housing, I had worked really hard to put it together. And they decided that [then Environment Secretary] Liz Truss would present it, who is a lovely woman, but she didn't know an awful lot about it. I kind of drilled in, and I thought: 'Well if they're not going to use me for that, it's the biggest symbol that I'm on my way out.' I had worked like hell on that, but I will always be grateful to David Cameron. He gave me five years. Not many people get five years in a top government department. He is quite entitled to have who he wants.

Somewhat to his surprise, Sir Eric found himself enjoying life on the back benches during his final two years in the Commons. A supporter of Theresa May during the 2016 leadership contest, he was appointed by her to serve as the government's anti-Semitism czar, a role he will continue out of Parliament.

He says: 'I always say this to people: "Did I like being a minister? Yes, I bloody loved being a minister. But I've just moved on, I've just got back into things." It was nice to have slightly more time.'

While he was tempted to stand again at the election,

he felt at sixty-five it was time to bow out gracefully. 'The election came as a shock,' he says.

I had decided I wasn't going to do another one. I could have done another term, I probably could have done another two terms, I could have done it, I think, with a degree of distinction. But you've got to say goodbye. I am young enough to do something else.

[Theresa May] has asked me to stay to do the [Special post-]Holocaust Envoy [position], which of course involves lots of international travelling, something I'm massively interested in, and I think I've actually made a really big difference. I've got the modern definition of anti-Semitism accepted by thirty-two countries, we're building [a] new museum and learning centre. I feel like I have got things to do. And I have never, ever, ever wanted to tread water. In truth, I've never been happier.

Sir Eric believes his envoy role is more relevant than ever before, given accusations that the Labour Party under Jeremy Corbyn is tolerant of anti-Semitism.

You know, there are lots of things wrong with the Labour Party, I fought it for most of my adult life, but I respected it. It is a great party. And what has happened to it is heart-breaking.

Listening to some of them who just don't get it, they think you can have a distinguished record of anti-racism and that covers you from being anti-Semitic. And it simply doesn't.

He is critical of both Mr Corbyn and Tim Farron, the Liberal Democrat leader, for failing to act more quickly and decisively against members who make anti-Semitic remarks.

'I don't know whether he's an anti-Semite or not,' he says of Mr Corbyn.

He has all these anti-racist policies, but what I do know is that he is very negligent about the issue and the company that he keeps, and the people that surround him. Ultimately it goes way up to the top.

I remember listening to old Farron talking about the procedural difficulties, how it took several weeks to get someone out. I removed someone from the party within twenty minutes. And the only reason it took that long was I couldn't get through to some of the members of the board. You've got to show absolute zero tolerance.

There was a Conservative councillor who said something more than unfortunate about travellers, and he was out, he was gone, he had to resign his seat. And that's the only way to do it.

If you compare that to the nonsense [Labour] went through with Ken Livingstone [over his claim Hitler was a Zionist], it's a prime example. People have to understand this – you can't play a part in politics if you're a bigot.

Sir Eric fears that the left has allowed anti-Semitic tones to enter the debate in a misguided attempt to woo Muslim communities. 'Part of it has been pandering to a growing Muslim vote in this country,' he says.

But the politics among the more strong Muslim groups, they're not like that.

There are some extremists but most people understand that British identity is made up of having a strong Jewish community, a strong Muslim community, a strong Hindu community, a strong Christian community, a strong non-believer community. That's what being British is.

Anybody can exploit, but politicians should be about bringing people together and showing leadership.

Sir Eric planned to spend the 2017 election in much the same way he has those of the past fifty years, 'knocking on doors on behalf of friends' in the party. He said election night itself would be a wrench, as would the following days.

'Of course I would very much like to be a Member of Parliament,' he says.

I will never again have those MP letters after my name – it's something that makes me very sad. But I've never been sentimental. I've never looked back and thought: 'Those were the glory days.' I've never said to friends: 'Ah, I was a minister…'

On the day that Parliament is formed and I'm not there, I will be full of angst. If I wasn't full of angst I should have given it up ten years ago. I will miss it like crazy.

I get really hacked off with people saying: 'Enjoy your retirement.' I'm not retiring, I'm just not going to be an MP. I'm sixty-five. I might retire when I'm eighty, but I'm not retiring now.

CV

Born and raised in Keighley, West Yorkshire, an employment consultant, chairman of the Young Conservatives and leader of Bradford Council.

1992   elected MP for Brentford & Ongar.
1993   becomes PPS at the Department of Industry, appointed vice-chairman of the Conservative Party.
1998   becomes shadow Social Security minister.
2001   becomes shadow Transport minister.
2002   becomes shadow Local Government minister.
2005   becomes deputy chairman of the Conservative Party.
2007   becomes shadow Communities Secretary.

2009   becomes chairman of the Conservative Party.

2010   becomes Communities Secretary.

2015   sacked from Cabinet, appointed Special Post-Holocaust Envoy, appointed Knight Batchelor.

2017   stands down from Parliament.

Married to Irene.

ALAN JOHNSON

Alan Johnson, 67, was Labour MP for Hull West & Hessle 1997–2017.

How did you end up in Parliament?
'It was arranged for me to be parachuted in to Hull West & Hessle. There was what was laughingly called an adoption meeting, but halfway through [the 1997 election campaign], they didn't have a lot of choice.'

How did you feel on first becoming an MP?
'We all felt, that Class of '97, like we were something special, because we had been out of power for eighteen years, and here we were occupying the government benches. There was this riot of colour which 100 new women [brought] to the House of Commons, as opposed to grey and dark blue suits.'

Best of times:

'It was genuinely getting the trawlermen everything they had been fighting for. They were incredible people. Talk about stoical; Hull lost 900 ships in 150 years of long-distance water trawling, 8,000 people lost, the most dangerous job in the world, a mortality rate seventeen times more than coal mining. To get them that compensation … was a sweet victory for me personally, it was a sweet victory for them, because they had dedicated their lives to this. [It showed] the importance of a Labour government, the importance of my role as a junior minister. It had to be the highest point of my political career.'

Worst of times:

'The electorate deciding they had had enough of us [in 2010]. I went from being Home Secretary to being shadow Home Secretary, having never been on the opposition benches. Suddenly I was there and it was weird because you always sat and saw the Speaker's right profile, and now you were sitting looking at his left profile. It was like *Alice through the Looking Glass*. And all that support has gone, all the civil servants have gone. They were the preserve of the person opposite me, who was Theresa May. And that was just particularly depressing.'

Why are you leaving?

'I hadn't quite made up my mind but I was moving towards

thinking, "Well, let's have that dilemma in 2020 whether to step down or not." But Theresa May decided I would have it three years earlier and then it seemed absolutely the right thing to do. Do I want five more years of this that takes me into my seventies, or do I want three more years, given that I probably would have gone in 2020, to do other things?'

What are your thoughts for future MPs?
'Look and observe and learn. Just gauge the mood of the place, find your way around, don't feel you have to constantly be standing up making speeches to be an effective parliamentarian. When you want to get the lie of the land and get a better feel for the place, go in and sit [in the Commons Chamber] for an afternoon and just listen and watch, because judging the mood of the place is very difficult.'

Do you have any regrets about leaving the Commons? And what are you going to do next?
'I didn't feel sad, I felt very happy because there's a really good woman, Emma Hardy, succeed[ing] me. She is a local primary school teacher. She said she joined the Labour Party because of me. It's very nice of her to say that. But the constituency is in safe hands, that's for sure.

There are jobs that I have been offered that I have turned

down, mainly because they are London-based and I will be living completely in East Yorkshire. Some charities have asked me to get involved. I've written a lot of articles. As long as it doesn't get in the way of my writing so I can meet my deadline for my publishers of January, which is when I have to hand in my [next] book.'

ALAN JOHNSON: THE FULL STORY

Alan Johnson's childhood, early life and political awakening are familiar to readers of his best-selling memoirs. He was brought up by his sister, Linda, after his father left the family and his mother passed away, when Alan was twelve and Linda just sixteen years old. He left school at fifteen and became a postman three years later. When he became a trade union representative in the Union of Communication Workers, he found his political calling. Rising to become general secretary, he was known as New Labour's favourite union boss. His entry into the House of Commons was both sudden and unexpected. The sitting MP in Hull West was among a number of older Members who had been tempted to stand aside with the offer of a seat in the House of Lords. Mr Johnson says he had not been manoeuvring to enter the Commons, and was surprised but intrigued when the call came through that a vacancy had opened up at short notice.

'It was halfway through the six-week '97 election [campaign],' he says.

So for three of those six weeks I was walking around Croydon [North] saying, 'Vote for Malcolm Wicks,' who was the local MP, and for the next three weeks I was walking around Hull West & Hessle saying, 'Vote for me'.

It wasn't a selection at all, I was parachuted in. I had to go through a silly interview with the NEC [national executive committee of the Labour Party]. I was on the NEC, so I was interviewed by my friends.

I was so late into the constituency, they didn't have any posters. They had posters for my predecessor who had stepped down to spend more time with his peerage. They found a candidate in Hessle, the guy who was the MP for a long period in the '50s and '60s, Jimmy Johnson, so there were some 'Vote Johnson' posters from that era which were hardly in tune with the kind of modern New Labour message that we wanted to send, but they were the only things we had.

And it was very, very difficult. The only thing was, I still had the support of the union, I was still the general secretary for a month or so until I had got elected, so I did have a support mechanism.

I remember it being a long period of trying to soak up information about this new patch stretching from the

Humber Bridge to the Myton Bridge across the River Hull, knocking on lots of doors and speaking to lots of people. There was no canvassing because it was a safe seat. I said: 'Well, where are the canvass returns? Where is the contact list? How do we know who our supporters are?' And [my agent], who is very sage, he said to me: 'Alan, don't worry, we'll win, just don't worry.' And I did. By the biggest majority ever by an MP in Hull. It was a landslide, the '97 victory. Nothing to do with my wisdom and sagacity, I had only been there three weeks. In fact, my majority went down in direct proportion to how familiar people were with me.

Despite the near-certain knowledge that he was about to become an MP, Mr Johnson approached election night of 1 May 1997 with a certain amount of trepidation:

Although everyone tells you you're safe, you do kind of think, 'What if something goes wrong?' So the actual announcement at three o'clock in the morning was very special to me. I remember that very well. To have been elected by people although they hardly knew me meant something to me.

Mr Johnson's memory of his first day in the Commons nearly twenty years ago also remains sharp.

I had a house in Upper Norwood which was just twenty minutes away from Westminster so I drove in. There was no real security pre-9/11. There was a copper on the gate who had a sheaf of photographs of new MPs, and there were hundreds of us. I gave my name, he looked at the photograph, looked at me, and he let us through. We got through the barrier and saw the directions to the underground car park but didn't know where to go from there.

Alongside me, just two places away in the underground car park as I was struggling to get out, [was] an open-topped, two-seater sports car with [notorious Conservative MP and diarist] Mr Alan Clark in it. He had been out of Parliament, he had lost his seat in '92, and he had come back. He kind of unfolded himself out of this open-topped sports car and I thought, 'Well, he knows where he's going, I'll follow him.'

He was absolutely languid, one hand in his pocket, he had no papers, pushing back his hair, totally au fait and at home with his surroundings, whereas I followed with briefcases and folders under my arm to find the way from the garage to where I was supposed to be in the House of Commons. He certainly felt he belonged there. I wasn't quite so sure I did.

As you come up from the car park, there is an escalator, and there is always a smell of burning rubber on that escalator. It was there twenty years ago and it's still there, and it always evokes that memory of my first time entering Parliament.

With his background as a senior trade unionist, Mr Johnson was to some extent familiar with the House of Commons, and already knew a number of MPs. But arriving with the magic letters after his own name was a different experience.

I had spent a lot of time in the place, but of course [had] never [been past] the two coppers who stand guarding the entrance to the Members' Lobby, I had never been to those places [past] the Central Lobby, the Strangers' Cafeteria.

I knew plenty of MPs, although this was a huge intake. There were 100-odd new women. Incredible to believe there were only twenty-five women out of 650 MPs before that May 1997 election. Because of all-women shortlists we transformed that situation. With disabled MP Anne Begg in her wheelchair, with more people from ethnic minorities – still not enough, but more women, more ethnic minorities – it was a huge change in the Chamber.

The Conservative Party, 167 MPs, they were reduced to a small rump sitting in a small corner of the Chamber. They didn't even fill the opposition benches.

So it was quite strange and exciting and exhilarating if you were in the Labour movement.

Despite the euphoria of joining the first Labour government for eighteen years, Mr Johnson found the practicalities of settling into the Commons problematic. 'It was awful,' he says.

You didn't have an office, you didn't have any staff and whilst the country was going through a general election and therefore there were no MPs, you can't expect the public to suddenly have no problems to contact their MPs about, so [there were] literally bundles of letters that had been sent to my predecessor. I had nowhere to put them. I had a key for an ancient locker along the corridors of the House of Commons. I don't know what happened to the key, I only used it once just to put these bundles of letters in there up until I got some kind of order in my life.

Eventually you get allocated an office. Mine was a horrible windowless one in the House of Commons. I think they thought because I had been a trade union general secretary that I should have a special favour that my office should be in the House of Commons. Which was fine, but an office without any windows, without any light, didn't suit me at all. I got out of there pretty quick.

It really was a difficult period which all MPs go through until they have got their feet under a desk and they have got an office and they're functioning properly and they have had their surgeries. The period before that is very disquieting.

Once he was set up with an office and staff, Mr Johnson found that he was a natural fit for an MPs' life. 'As for the House itself, being a trade union representative is a good apprenticeship because we follow formality and procedure,' he says.

> We are used to dealing with individual problems, that's what trade unions do, not just collectively, individually, we have our legal and medical services giving people advice on any issue under the sun. So surgeries I was used to, standing up and talking I was used to, making representation I was used to, writing letters I was used to, and dealing with procedures.
>
> The only difference is, of course, the House of Commons Chamber is a forum like no other for speaking. There are no niceties, you don't get a table in front of you, don't get a glass of water.
>
> Someone said to Churchill, 'What's it like facing the enemy?' He said: 'No, I'm facing the opposition, the enemy are behind me.' It's a forum that is built for confrontation. It's quite a disconcerting place to give a speech, particularly a maiden speech.

Mr Johnson had arrived in Parliament with a clear mission. During his brief campaign in Hull, he had become aware of a long-running injustice involving local fishermen. He says:

West Hull was the once the biggest long-distance water fishing port in the world, and the men there had been treated disgracefully, told they were casual workers, and not even entitled to statutory redundancy.

The reason that they lost their jobs was because the British government agreed with the Icelandic government after the so-called Cod Wars that there should be a 200-mile limit around the coast of Iceland. That was the end of long-distance water trawling. So that was a cause I was able to take up immediately, what I called the biggest industrial injustice I had ever come across.

Mr Johnson's determination to win compensation for his constituents meant he came close to missing out on a ministerial career when, soon after entering the Commons, he was invited to become parliamentary private secretary to Dawn Primarolo, the Financial Secretary to the Treasury.

'I turned it down,' he says.

Nick Brown, [the] Chief Whip, had to sit me down and have a conversation with me because there was this burning injustice of the trawlermen's compensation.

I wasn't ambitious. I was ambitious to be general secretary of my trade union, [but] once I decided to leave that, change careers, I wanted to be a good MP. To me, that was a good constituency MP; very important to me.

[As] a PPS, getting on the ministerial ladder, albeit the lowest rung, you can't speak in the Commons any more, you can't put down early day motions, you can't have adjournment debates, you can't question ministers. You're now part of the executive, and that was my argument to Nick Brown: I have only been in the Commons for seven months, this was going to inhibit my ability to represent my constituents.

Nick patiently explained to me … that it's recognised that you can't have those kind of advantages being able to talk from the floor so you get a compensating access to ministers and civil servants that you wouldn't have as a backbencher, and the two kind of cancel each other out.

From the inside, he was able to help secure the trawlermen all the compensation they had requested.

Once he had been assured that joining the government would not harm the trawlermen's campaign, Mr Johnson was happy to see his career take off, and admits he had an 'obvious desire' to become a full minister, which he did two years later, at the Department for Trade and Industry. He found his newly elevated status had little impact in the constituency.

'Constituents never knew what job I was doing in government,' he says.

They didn't follow politics that closely; why should they? When I was Health Secretary, a woman came to my surgery, and pleaded with me to write a letter on her behalf to the Secretary of State for Health. I was the Secretary of State for Health, so that was no problem.

Life on the government benches suited him. 'I enjoyed it,' he says.

I enjoyed it completely. The difference between being in government and being in opposition is huge. It must have been so depressing for Labour MPs who came in in the election of 1979, to spend eighteen years [in opposition], and by the time we were back in power, lots of those careers had gone.

So I wanted to spend all my time on the government benches because I recognised how futile it was just being in opposition and going through the charade of shadowing ministers. Once you are in government and you have got the civil service working for you, you can really start making a difference to people's lives. So I loved being a minister. Seven months in I was part of the executive and stayed part of the executive for the next thirteen years.

In 2004, Mr Johnson joined the Cabinet at the Department for Work and Pensions, the first of a series of big jobs which took him pinging around Whitehall at a dizzying speed.

Seen as a safe pair of hands who could be trusted to sort out troubled departments, he served in five senior Cabinet positions in just six years and admits it became a frustration that he was not able to remain in post for longer.

Throughout his early years in Cabinet, politics was dominated by the ever-present tensions between Tony Blair and his Chancellor and successor-in-waiting, Gordon Brown. Mr Johnson says:

> It was difficult. I didn't want to be seen as a Blairite or a Brownite, I just wanted to get on with my job. I thought they were two incredibly talented people, the Lennon and McCartney of Labour politics, and I couldn't understand why Gordon – you have to blame Gordon – had such a terrible attitude. He was in such a strop almost continuously with Tony. And of course it was because he felt Tony should be moving on. I was right in the middle of all that, I was Education Secretary when all that came to a head. You have to be pleasant and conciliatory on both sides and stand your ground when you need to stand your ground.

When Mr Brown finally took over, in June 2007, Mr Johnson's impartiality was rewarded with promotion to Health Secretary. He says:

> I stayed two years there and that was a luxury, that

probably was the happiest time, not least because we were celebrating the sixtieth anniversary of the NHS.

We were spending the right amount of money, 9 per cent of GDP, which was the European average. We were getting really good results on things like psychological therapies; transforming mental health; the satisfaction rate for people in hospitals was [the] highest ever known. It was an extraordinarily good time to be in Health.

Mr Johnson ended his ministerial career in one of the great offices of state, as Home Secretary. He says:

You can't say the Home Office is enjoyable, because it's 24/7, you're dealing with so many terrible things which you can never talk about, let alone relate to, and you're the voice for people who are doing all kinds of heroic things but can never have any kind of public profile.

You're that democratic link. So the security forces need to do something, you're the one who has to sign it off, which means you have to make yourself available every minute of the day and night. And your freedom is curtailed because you can't walk to the corner shop to get a newspaper without these five armed guards with you. I didn't enjoy that bit of it. But I enjoyed the intellectual challenge.

Mr Johnson is often spoken of as Labour's lost leader, a

charge he rejects, although he admits there was a time, following the 2010 general election which resulted in a hung parliament, when he thought he might possibly be about to become Prime Minister.

> I would have done it in 2010 if the coalition had come off when we talked to the Lib Dems, because Gordon would have stepped down and we needed someone to step forward. We planned [for me] to do three years to get through the worst of that [hung parliament]. Why waste your young talent on that?

Instead, as the Liberal Democrats formed a coalition with the Conservatives, and Labour went into opposition after thirteen years in office, Mr Johnson threw his weight behind David Miliband in the ensuing leadership contest, only to see him pipped at the post by his younger brother, Ed. 'I was very committed to David Miliband,' Mr Johnson says.

> I think I announced his candidature before he did. I went on the *Today* programme and was asked if I was going to run for leader. I said: 'No, I'm backing David Miliband.'
> That seemed to me to be absolutely right. I had just turned sixty, which is young in political terms of these days, but I had done thirteen years on the front bench, I kind of fancied doing different things. And there was this golden

talent, and indeed his brother Ed. [There were other] very talented people there who were capable of taking a lead; Yvette Cooper, I have always been a very big supporter of Yvette, and many of the other women who have come through the system since '97 were in the running. So I didn't see myself as being the right leader in 2010.

Following the election of Ed Miliband in October 2010, Mr Johnson made a rare misstep by accepting the post of shadow Chancellor. He found himself unequipped for the task of shadowing George Osborne, and after a difficult time in his private life, when it emerged that his then-wife had been involved in a relationship with his police bodyguard, he stepped down from the post after just four months.

Describing the period following the 2010 general election as his worst in Parliament, he says:

Shadowing my own department as a shadow Home Secretary was bad enough. Shadow Chancellor, [with] no help or assistance there – it was the very early days – coming in with an absence of any kind of coherent support system, was really difficult. People do it, and they do it well, they do it much better than I can do it. I just wasn't cut out [for it]. It was the wrong job for me as we soon discovered.

Leaving the front bench meant Mr Johnson could reacquaint himself with the Commons, and gave him the time and leisure to observe some rising stars up close. One he is unimpressed with is Boris Johnson, favourite to succeed Theresa May as Tory leader. He says:

> [The Commons] is a very difficult place. The jokes that Boris Johnson makes elsewhere die a death in the Chamber. Humour is a very important part of the speeches, but it is such a formalised environment that the things that are funny are usually the stuff that is spontaneous and not the things that are planned. Certainly no one has affection for a court jester, it's not really going to get you very far.

Alan Johnson is conscious that he himself lacks the killer instinct to have become leader – and is content with that, despite the continued entreaties from his supporters through his final years in Parliament to stand.

> Sometimes I feel guilty about that, because people say you should put the party first. The party, to me, it's an institution. How can you love an institution? It's people that matter to me, so there is a kind of fear of letting the side down. But I just know that I wouldn't be happy doing it. If I wasn't happy doing it, it would show. So what's the point? You should only run for a leader if you have got

the passion to do that job. Thank God there are people like that.

Maybe Gordon [Brown] should have thought different-ly about it. He was such a talented man but that whole showbiz side of it, you've got to be on display, you're under scrutiny. Tony [Blair] was a bit of an actor, and he could do that, he took all of that in his stride, but having seen them do it and having seen pressures on them, made me even more determined that that's not what I wanted and so I have never regretted it, not for a minute. And inci-dentally, I don't think the party would be in any better or worse shape [under my leadership].

Mr Johnson is not convinced that, even had he run, he would have been successful in the most recent leadership contest, particularly given the changing face of the party membership, with tens of thousands of people signing up as supporters to elect the left-winger Jeremy Corbyn as leader.

'I don't think anyone would have beaten Jeremy Corbyn in 2015,' he says.

There was a complete mood change, and there [were] the £3 members coming in. It was almost like we became two parties very quickly.

This personality cult around Jeremy; he never troubled himself with making any compromises and he had always been a backbencher and that seemed to me to be what people were looking for. They wouldn't have found that in me. So I don't think I would have stood any chance of winning even if I had put my name forward.

As someone on the right of the party, he has felt increasingly out of place in Corbyn's Labour Party and, while it is not the only or even the main reason he is standing down, he did not relish the prospect of remaining a Labour MP under the current leadership. Despite the show of unity following the better-than-expected result in the general election, he remains suspicious of the impact of the so-called Corbynistas on the party, and particularly of Momentum, the grassroots movement created to support Mr Corbyn.

This whole idea that you have this rather sinister-sounding Momentum waiting in the wings, I think it will very soon turn ugly. People will be judged on whether they are purist enough in their support for the 'Great Leader'. You are going to get all that we saw in the early '80s with Militant.

This idea that people have to be involved day to day, not just at election time – this is the party trying to get MPs to do what the party wants them to do and lose their individual judgement on these issues, not work for their constituents but work for a small clique; all of that is going to happen. All of that will be very distasteful. I could see that happening.

'I think there are problems to face, but he did well,' he adds of the election result.

There is something happening out there, and I shall enjoy it from the side lines. Even if there had been a transformation and we were being led by a British version of [the new centrist French President Emmanuel] Macron, [and] we were heading for a huge and stunning victory, I still would have stepped down.

The main reason Mr Johnson is leaving the Commons now is to pursue his increasingly absorbing career as a writer. His three volumes of memoirs are all bestsellers as well as being critically acclaimed, and he is now turning his hand to fiction. 'The writing has just been a joy,' he says.

The real challenge for me is writing fiction and not falling flat on my face, so that's something I am really looking forward to. It's time to go off and do different things. And it's really good to go when people are saying: 'I'm really sorry you're going,' rather than: 'What, is he still doing that?'

Always the trade union rep, what few regrets Mr Johnson has about leaving the Commons are for his employees.

> The thing about standing down is your staff lose their jobs and I feel terrible about it. Telling my people in 2020 I'll probably be moving on and giving them time is one thing; telling them in two weeks' time, that's all we get, two weeks and the office is closed, everything has got to be moved out and they have not got anywhere to work anymore, [although] they get paid for a bit longer than that, it's pretty sudden.

For himself, Mr Johnson's only wobble came on the day of his departure.

> When I felt strange was walking out of my office in One Parliament Street, when I had to hand my pass in, had to hand my key in and walk out the door and catch the No. 3 bus to Crystal Palace from Whitehall. That felt very strange because I knew I would never be going back in.
>
> You get a pass as a Member, for the rest of your life you can walk in, [but] would you really want to go in there? What, for a cup of coffee? Just to sit around looking at MPs doing their job?
>
> There is that terrible division in the House of Commons

between MPs and strangers, so in a sense you would be going back as a stranger. All those areas you can't walk through, the Members' Cloakroom, the Members' Lobby. As the coppers were saying, 'Goodbye Sir', or 'Goodbye Alan Johnson MP', it was: 'You're a stranger now.' I thought: 'I don't ever want to come back here now.' I want to be there as it was, as a Member, not some kind of half, hybrid ex-Member.

But in a way it was good that it was sudden. Because if I had been working up to it I might have been a bit more distraught about it. I wasn't distraught at all as it happened. Fine, life moves on. Things move forward. It was nice while it lasted.

CV

Born west London, postman and trade union leader.

- 1997 elected MP for Hull West & Hessle, becomes PPS to Dawn Primarolo at the Treasury.
- 1999 becomes junior minister, Department of Trade and Industry.
- 2001 becomes Minister of State for Employment.
- 2003 becomes Minister of State for Education.
- 2004 becomes Work and Pensions Secretary.
- 2005 becomes Trade and Industry Secretary.

2006 becomes Education Secretary.
2007 unsuccessfully stands for deputy leadership; becomes Health Secretary.
2009 becomes Home Secretary.
2010 becomes shadow Home Secretary; becomes shadow Chancellor.
2011 resigns from shadow Cabinet.
2017 stands down from Parliament.

Married to Carolyn, four children from previous relationships.

SIR ALAN HASELHURST

Sir Alan Haselhurst, 80, was Conservative MP for Middleton & Prestwich 1970–74 and Saffron Walden 1977–2017.

How did you end up in Parliament?
'In 1967, the phone rang in my office, and they said: "This is the Middleton & Prestwich Conservative Association and we are looking for a candidate."'

How did you feel on first becoming an MP?
'I was obviously thrilled to bits. I had worked the patch very hard to secure my election in the first place and I was desperate to do well on [my constituents'] behalf. It was a dream come true. It was what I wanted to do. I really took to it.'

Best of times:

'The highest point was becoming chairman of the Ways and Means Committee [Deputy Speaker]. It was a total surprise. I was staggered because I'd never thought of it. I managed to do it for thirteen years which was some sort of record.'

Worst of times:

'The lowest [moment in the Commons] was not becoming Speaker. That sounds arrogant, but it isn't meant to be. Obviously you felt you had a chance at the speakership, so it was disappointing not to get it, having come so close to the flame.'

Why are you leaving?

'I am eighty next month. I don't feel it, but that's the truth. Mrs May has rather wrecked my timing, in that having been elected in 2015 to serve another Parliament, of course we expected that to be until 2020. I just felt the balance had tipped slightly, with those three extra years, and came to the conclusion that perhaps I should step down now.'

What are your thoughts for future MPs?

'The first two years in the constituency are absolutely critical because if you build the foundation then something very extraordinary or stupid has got to happen for you to be imperilled. If you don't get it right to start with you may have all sorts of difficulty as time goes on.'

Do you have any regrets about leaving the Commons? And what are you going to do next?

'I am sad to go. I've tried to avoid being too emotional about it. I've had a fantastic innings, I've been so lucky, I've loved every minute of it. I feel I did some good things. I'm just now thinking about the next phase of my life. I just don't want to curl up and do nothing. I will wait and see if anybody comes calling. I don't think I want a life just watching cricket.'

SIR ALAN HASELHURST: THE FULL STORY

Sir Alan Haslehurst insists he was 'absolutely not' from a political family. His father was a retail pharmacist, and, at the outset, he says it was his background which made him a Conservative. 'My parents always used to encourage me to take an interest in what was in the newspapers and I was always a bit of a talker,' he says.

I was just brought up, I think, as a Conservative. I just assumed [I would be]. Of course, Churchill was the big hero to me. I was old enough to listen to some of his wartime broadcasts. [I] went to boarding school in 1951 just as a general election was taking place. There was great excitement. A mock election was taking place in the school and I took an interest in that.

Sir Alan went on to win a place at Oxford's Oriel College, which at the time did not have a Conservative Association. He says:

Over a weekend therefore I became the Conservative rep in Oriel College. It all took off from there. I became absolutely immersed in Oxford politics and was quite clear by the time I left Oxford, as a very different Conservative from the way I started – by then I did actually know why I believed in the Conservative Party – that what I wanted if possible was to get into Parliament. The question was, how on earth to go about it?

Having originally thought he would become a barrister, as Sir Alan's time at university drew to a close he began to realise the law was not for him. A friend suggested he go into industry, and he ended up with a job at ICI Plastics. At the same time, eager to further his political career, he joined the Young Conservatives. Rising through the ranks during the 1960s, he became first a branch chairman then constituency chairman in the area he had made his home after Oxford, Welwyn Garden City, mainly, he claims, because no one else wanted the job. By 1966 he had become national chairman of the Young Conservatives, a role which gave him a high profile, including, as it did, an invitation to speak at the party's annual conference. Soon afterwards, he applied to go on the Conservatives' candidates' list, and was accepted.

Before Sir Alan could begin to think about applying for seats, however, fate intervened in the form of a phone call from the chairman of the Middleton & Prestwich Conservative Association, a marginal seat in Greater Manchester. 'I couldn't remember what the majority was,' he says.

There were a lot of double-barrelled constituencies around the Greater Manchester area, most of which were not held by the Conservatives after '66. I thought, well, I could dally, but do I want to try, whether it's a 19,000 Labour majority or a 5,000 majority? I said, 'Yes, I've got to start somewhere.' And, blow me, it was a 3,800 majority. I went for interview in a fairly relaxed state of mind thinking this is going to be the start of a long, long road, and was chosen. I was elected by just over 1,000, which I lost in February 1974 by 500.

Sir Alan's election in a highly marginal seat in June 1970 meant his first years in Parliament were dominated by his need to cultivate his constituency in order to survive the next election – an endeavour which was ultimately unsuccessful.

As he arrived for his first day, however, he could have no idea he would still be there nearly fifty years later. 'I hadn't been to Parliament much,' he says of his first impressions.

> I think I'd only sat in the [public] gallery, when Rab Butler was the Leader of the House of Commons. On the day that I arrived as an elected Member, I was coming down with a close friend of mine who had similarly been elected in the north-west, and we talked about sharing a secretary because the allowance in those days was pretty meagre, so you had to share. And we realised we didn't know, as Members, the way in. We knew the public entrance but we didn't know which way you went in as a Member. Someone who knew us both, who was an old hand, then arrived on the scene and said: 'What are you two reprobates doing here?' And we said, 'We just wondered which way we go in.' 'So I'll show you,' he said. And that was how we first started. There is much more effort to organise the induction of new Members these days.

Sir Alan's election coincided with the end of six years of Labour rule and the arrival of Edward Heath as Prime Minister. He says:

> It was exciting from my point of view that we had a Conservative government led by Heath, who I'd known for a

number of years because he had been one of a generation of Conservative politicians who had really made some impact on the politics of Oxford during the years that I was there. I had also known him through the Federation of Conservative Students. We were all backing him.

Within a few months of his election, Sir Alan was invited to take the first step on the ministerial ladder, when Francis Pym, then the party's Chief Whip, telephoned to ask him to become parliamentary private secretary to Richard Sharples, the Minister of State at the Home Office. Eighteen months later, Sharples left to become governor of Bermuda (where he would be assassinated), and Sir Alan served as PPS to his successor, Mark Carlisle. As the parliament drew to a close, Sir Alan was promoted to PPS to the Home Secretary, Robert Carr. Unfortunately for him, and in a forerunner of Theresa May's strategic error forty-three years later in calling an early general election, in February 1974, three months after Sir Alan had begun working for Carr, Mr Heath gambled on going to the country early.

'And then I lost my seat,' Sir Alan says.

The February election, I felt, was a mistake. Mark Carlisle and Robert Carr and people I respected were also only slowly dragged into believing we had to do it. I never thought we had to do it. I thought it was a ghastly mistake. And so it proved.

Brian Harrison [MP for Maldon] said to me as I was leaving the dining room for the last time before dissolution, 'Good luck Alan, but don't take this the wrong way, you might be better off if you lose.' Of course I bridled at that. I thought no, I'm determined to keep Middleton & Prestwich. But in the circumstances that prevailed, I lost it. And I came to realise, slowly, that what Brian Harrison had said was right, although the three and a half years I had out of the House at the time stretched. The other thing about February '74 was that I was unemployed.

From the moment of his defeat, Sir Alan dedicated himself to finding a new seat – a determination which made his search for a job to pay the bills until he could return to Parliament problematic, as potential employers demanded he give up his political ambitions. 'I didn't want that. I wanted desperately to get back,' he says.

I've always said that the people who never get into Parliament, despite all their valiant effort, are not in the same position as someone who has been in, known what it is like, loved every minute of it, and [is] desperate to get back. What I missed was terrible, whereas if you hadn't been in, hadn't missed it, perhaps it wasn't as bad.

I kept away from Westminster. I had friends who had got in in 1970 and had survived 1974. One of them said to me: 'Come and have lunch.' I said, 'Well, I don't know.' He said, 'Don't be ridiculous, come and have lunch in Strangers' Dining Room.' It was a gut-wrenching experience as far as I was concerned. It had been over two years since I'd been there. Every member of staff down to the waitresses and waiters in the Strangers' Dining Room, the police officers on duty, said to me, 'Oh hello, Mr Haselhurst. When are you coming back?' The fact that I was remembered in that way, and then the great love that the staff of the building have about the place where they work, that for a time made it even tougher until probably a year later when finally my ball rolled into the slot of Saffron Walden.

Fortuitously, Sir Alan's time out of the Commons proved shorter than he had feared. He says:

There were thirty-three vacancies in Conservative seats for one reason or another, either death or retirement at the following election that was to be. And I applied, of course, for every one of them. Eleven didn't bother giving me an interview. Of the twenty-two which did, I got on to, in total, eleven shortlists, the eleventh being [the] fortunate one. And then Brian Harrison's words came home to me and have come home to me ever since, because some of my best chums and most important rivals, if you like, trying to get a safe seat in Parliament were waiting on '79 or whenever the election was going to come. Suddenly, in Saffron Walden, I was pitched into a by-election through the untimely death of Sir Peter Kirk at the age of forty-eight. I was then in Parliament two years before they got there.

When he returned to the House of Commons, in July 1977, Sir Alan found it a changed place, with Margaret Thatcher now party leader and his hero Ted Heath glowering on the back benches. Any hopes he might have entertained of returning to the government seemed to have faded. 'My star never particularly prospered under Mrs Thatcher's leadership period,' he says.

I don't think my face fitted. I thought it was a bit unfair, but I was branded one of the Wets. I was on that wing of the Conservative Party, and I think there was always that suspicion of people who had been there under Ted Heath's leadership. You were seen as part of the *ancien régime*. It would be a lie to say I wasn't particularly ambitious, but I began to realise that I'd rather been overtaken by that absence when Margaret Thatcher was building the party, to have moulded it around her, as it were. People had made advances and been given posts.

When Thatcher's long leadership came to an end in 1990, and she was succeeded by John Major, Sir Alan was resigned to life on the back benches – and had come to relish the other ways that MPs could make an impact in Parliament.

Probably I wasn't the young hopeful by the time John Major became Prime Minister. I was perfectly relaxed about it because I was realistic. If it was not going to happen, it was not going to happen. But I still very much enjoyed the constituency side of things, representing that seat in particular.

From the start of his second spell in Parliament, Sir Alan felt like he had been given a precious opportunity to begin his political life over again. During his time in the Young Conservatives, he had met Rab Butler, the great Conservative Chancellor and Home Secretary, who had advised him that if he became an MP he should ensure he spent his first two years nurturing his constituency. 'That advice I remembered and I was determined, having fought, won and lost a marginal seat, that I was going to make absolutely damn sure to lay the foundations in Saffron Walden,' he says.

I had got this second chance in a fantastic constituency which was very large geographically. And I had also put my time out of the House to good use in that my social life had resumed [and] I had found someone I wanted to marry. I had got involved in voluntary organisations and I'd also for a brief period become chairman of a sports club. All these had enriched my life. Whilst it was a painful severance from Parliament in '74, it was very important to me that I had three years of normal life in which I did normal things. We had hardly been married more than a few months when I was chosen for Saffron Walden.

We were hoping for a family, which duly came along. I was absolutely determined that I was not going to let Saffron Walden slip through my fingers if I could possibly help it. I was going to build a foundation there and at the same time establish a good foundation to my marriage and enjoy my children and not be an absentee father, because of the hours the House used to keep on those days.

So I would come back pretty well every night, even though I had got accommodation in London. There was a sort of rule that if it was later than two o'clock in the morning, then probably not, because sometimes occasionally there were night sittings in those days. And therefore the children would see me in the morning, and I would see the children, even if I wasn't there to read them a bedtime story in the evening.

On election night 1997, as the Major government came

to a crashing end with the first Blair landslide, Sir Alan found that his hard work in the constituency had paid off. He says:

In '97, there was an enormous cull of the Conservative Party. My dear friend Tony Newton, who happened to be the Member for Braintree, the neighbouring constituency, had a 16,000 majority. I learned at two o'clock in the morning that he had lost. My majority from the 1992 election was 17,000 and a cold chill began to grip me. But the good people of Saffron Walden in fact returned me with a majority of 10,500. How lucky indeed I was.

To his surprise, 1997 also marked an uptick in Sir Alan's career, when, to his 'total surprise', he was invited to become chairman of the Ways and Means Committee – parliamentary speak for the post of Deputy Speaker of the House of Commons.

Come '97, when the party was at a very low ebb, I came up for the swearing in and I nipped into the opposition Whips' Office, concerned as much as anything else about what accommodation I might expect. On my way home I wanted to call in at the Waterstones bookshop at the corner of Trafalgar Square. I was in Waterstones when my mobile phone rang: Andrew Mackay. He was deputy whip at the time, and I had said 'Hi' to him when I was in the opposition Whips' Office. I couldn't understand why he was ringing me. Had I left something behind? Or was it something about accommodation? [There was poor] mobile phone reception, and I couldn't digest what he said about 'Deputy Speaker'. So I went out into Trafalgar Square and then I heard what he said: 'You are in line to be Deputy Speaker.' I must have looked a complete gawp to people who happened to have watched me at that particular moment.

I went home and I said [to my wife], 'You never know what's happened, they want me to be the Deputy Speaker.' Her words were: 'Go for it, you've had nothing else.' Which wasn't quite fair.

Sir Alan found he loved the job from the beginning – although his first few days were nerve-racking. 'The nervousness of it to start with,' he says.

The Leader of the House goes to the despatch box at 2.30 on the first day and says 'I beg to move that XY and Z are chairman of Ways and Means, first deputy, and second deputy.' Then, two hours later, I, as the senior one of the three, was in the chair!

The first task of course is to know everybody's name. With the intake the scale there was on the Labour side in particular, of course, [that] was quite hard work, but I did it. I felt my way. That's when you realise how helpful the clerks are, although the geography of the House, with them sitting with their backs to you, [means] you having to crane forward, they having to turn round and crane their necks, and sometimes, *sotto voce*, suggest what you might say if you were feeling perplexed. After a while certain things became more familiar and people were kind enough to say I did it with a certain elan.

In his new role, Sir Alan worked closely with Betty Boothroyd, the Labour MP who had been Speaker since 1992. He says:

We had never had much dealings with each other. My relationship with her had been wholly formal in the sense that I would go up to the chair when she was Deputy Speaker or Speaker to enquire whether or not I had a chance of being called in the debate, no more than that. But we were both Yorkshire people and we actually got on very well. We still do to this day.

In his thirteen years as Deputy Speaker, Sir Alan came to relish the Commons and his role within it, and gained an unparalleled antennae for the mood of the Chamber. He says:

It was a huge honour. I always had a feeling about the House of Commons. I'm not one of those people who was just there to shout at the other side. I had my political convictions which I was prepared to stand up and defend, [but] there are people who do it aggressively and there are people who do it in, they hope, a more reasoned way. I'm someone who is on the whole consensual. You get to know and respect some of the people on the other side of the House.

The House of Commons has a sort of abstract feeling about. You can be as stupid as you like in terms of putting forward an argument, if the House of Commons likes you it doesn't matter. But if you give the impression that, I'm bright and intelligent and you really want to be paying attention to what I'm saying, and come to the House for convenience rather than a sense of belonging, [you] don't fare quite so well. I've seen it happen on occasion where there might be someone who is rather favoured as a champion who has made an absolute fool of themself, and yet it doesn't matter the next day, everything is back to normal. You need goodwill in the House of Commons to proceed; that applies to the people who get to the very highest office.

When Mrs Boothroyd relinquished the Speakership in 2000, Sir Alan had every hope – and expectation – that as her deputy he might replace her. It was not to be.

'The Labour Party were just in no mood to have a Conservative when she announced her retirement,' he says. 'It's true it had alternated [until] that point; in fact it was a Conservative majority that chose Betty in '92. I think the view of the Labour Party was: we are 419, the Conservatives are 165, why the hell should we give them anything?'

To his surprise, Sir Alan gradually realised that, even had Labour supported him, a number of MPs on the Conservative side were opposed to him becoming Speaker. He says:

> I think the Tories were cross with me in 2000. They thought I had been too heavy on them. There may have been more bad behaviour on the part of a very much reduced numerically opposition. I, at the same time, was trying to make it clear that I was not afraid to chastise my own side, but they probably got the impression that I was being unfair to them. This was never deliberate on my side, other than to try to be fair, to be seen to be fair, but I think they felt that they bore rather more of the scars.

After 2000, Sir Alan stepped up his efforts to be accepted by both sides of the House. 'You were aware that you might be coming down more heavily on what might be perceived as "your side",' he says.

> If I had to reprove someone on the Conservative side for

something they had done, I was desperate to find an opportunity to do the same to someone on the government side to show that I was not trying to behave in any kind of partial way. I remember one colleague saying to me after my first failed attempt at the Speakership: 'We like Mark Two Haselhurst more than we like Mark One.' Now, in my second phase, I had settled into the job, and was doing it better.

The growing regard for Sir Alan on all sides of the House encouraged him to hope once again that he might become Speaker, following the forced resignation of Mrs Boothroyd's successor, Michael Martin, during the 2009 MPs' expenses scandal. Again he was disappointed. His candidacy was not helped by the decision of Sir George Young, then a senior shadow Cabinet member, to throw his cap into the ring. 'The affection for George Young meant that my side of the House was divided, which wasn't good,' Sir Alan says.

I myself had an admiration for George Young. But by then obviously I'd hoped that having served for twelve years as the senior Deputy that I had established something of a reputation for handling things alright. [I] got through fourteen Budgets without chaos. But no, they were divided, the Labour Party was still in a majority, and it didn't work out. Was that a low? Well, yes, maybe, a bit, but the high was actually being given the position. To be the chairman of the Ways and Means in the House of Commons in our country was a great honour.

With the election of John Bercow, a Conservative, as Speaker, Sir Alan felt he should abide by the convention that the Deputy is drawn from a different party, and so stepped down from the post he loved. He put his last years in Parliament to good use, first chairing the Commons Commonwealth Parliamentary Association and then the International Association a year later. In his role as chairman of the Administration Committee he oversaw attempts to modernise the Commons, cutting the dining subsidy in half and substantially boosting the numbers of visitors to Westminster.

In 2013, with the 2015 election on the horizon, he detected the first hints that some in his local party were beginning to feel it might be time for him to retire. 'I had a little bother, there was a little bit of stirring going on. One or two were plotting, on age grounds,' he says.

When we started to go into it, it turned out that it was not actually the case that there was a great wave of desire for change. I was then facing the general election and we got the biggest majority the constituency has ever had. That rather disproved the rumbling that we needed someone who could appeal to the younger voters, new ideas, new face – not at all.

Nonetheless, with his eightieth birthday approaching, Sir Alan conceded that his time in the Commons was coming to a close. He discussed the matter with his association chairman, and they agreed he would announce his departure in 2018, when new boundary changes would have taken effect. The early election called by Theresa May in April 2017 threw those plans into disarray.

'Mrs May's announcement took us all by surprise,' he says.

My first reaction was: I feel fine, everything is alright, we will carry on. A very important parliament will be formed, and I would be keen to be part of it. Then [I thought]: are there not now going to be people who will say, 'Oh come on Alan. This is now stretching it too far'? An old chum of mine happened to ring me that fateful week and said: 'Add five years to your age, Alan, that's how they will see it. And try to envisage you being their Member of Parliament when you're touching eighty-five.'

If you reach that sort of age, what you need to carry on [is] the wholehearted support of your party. That was an issue then. The best analysis I could do, the people I talked to, headcounts of the people who mattered, I probably would have won the selection but it would have been a more even choice this time. The week I spent moving from initial enthusiasm to 'nothing's wrong' to 'Well, maybe I'm kidding myself' – that was a bad week. But once I made up my mind, I was relaxed about it.

As he prepared to say goodbye to the Commons, in April 2017, Sir Alan was given the honour of asking the last question at Prime Minister's Questions before the general election. He says:

I was terribly nervous because I was worried my emotions would overcome me or that my voice might break, because I realised it was going to be the last words I would have ever uttered in the House. Fortunately, I managed to hold it together. And I could go out on a high as opposed to a low. There are a number of things which I achieved in that last parliament which I'm proud of.

Even as he celebrates his eightieth birthday, Sir Alan is not ready to retire completely.

The wisdom is, if you have had a very active life, it's a big mistake to stop completely. You do risk then your brain [going]. I obviously don't want that, so I need to be engaged in something. But, sensibly, at a slightly less hectic pace than I have known for the last forty years.

CV

Born in Yorkshire, executive for pharmaceutical firm ICI.

1964   elected chair of the Young Conservatives.

1970   elected MP for Middleton & Prestwich, becomes PPS at Home Office.

1973   becomes PPS to Robert Carr, Home Secretary.

1974   fails to be re-elected in Middleton & Prestwich.

1977   elected MP for Saffron Walden.

1979   becomes PPS to Mark Carlisle.

1997   becomes Deputy Speaker.

2000   stands unsuccessfully to become Speaker.

2009   stands unsuccessfully to become Speaker.

2010   returns to back benches.

2017   stands down from Parliament.

Married to Angela, three children.

GRAHAM ALLEN

Graham Allen, 64, was Labour MP for Nottingham North 1987–2017.

How did you end up in Parliament?

'A Conservative had won Nottingham North in 1983. I became a candidate in 1987. I had the big advantage of being born in the constituency, but also, having been away for one to two years, I came in as the local boy but also the outsider.'

How did you feel on first becoming an MP?

'I wasn't star-struck by Saint Stephen's Entrance, I had an agenda for reform. Very early on I had got a view about how it could change, not just the Parliamentary Labour Party, but Parliament as a whole.'

Best of times:

'Being an assiduous constituency MP for the area in which you were born, which means looking after the people who are on a very low incomes and need a strong defender. Early Years Intervention is the most important policy of my thirty years in the House of Commons. And having a strategic long-term view of where our democracy is to go if it is to remain a democracy.'

Worst of times:

'Iraq was a low point. It did seem obvious to me that this really was not the way to go. To invade another country and open the Pandora's box of religious hatred and bomb the hell out of people [was] really not the way that we should be exercising political power in this day and age. It seemed to me to be a big mistake. It seemed to me to be politically throwing away a lot of credibility. It was a terrible personal misjudgement by the Prime Minister.'

Why are you leaving?

'I was very happy to carry on to 2020 but I've got a weird joint problem called haemochromatosis, which means too much iron in the blood. Mrs May disposes of the Acts of Parliament for a fixed term, then demonstrates Parliament's pathetic response to any pressure from the executive by calling a vote to hold an early election. That was [on a] Tuesday;

on the Wednesday I'm up for it, I'm going to go for it again, then I have a long chat finishing about 3.15 a.m. with my wife, and my decision on the back of that discussion was not to go again, which was an incredibly difficult one.'

What are your thoughts for future MPs?
'Involve people, and insulate people and inoculate people from populism. Develop a strong democracy.'

Will you have any regrets on 8 June? And what are you going to do next?
'It is a little bit too early to say. My decision [to leave] had been taken very quickly. The longer it goes on, the more clear I am that I have made the right decision.'

GRAHAM ALLEN: THE FULL STORY

Graham Allen was born into a working-class family in Nottingham with a strong early link to the Labour Party. His father was a coal miner, his mother a textile worker, and they were ambitious for him to do well at school and go to university, hopes which he initially disappointed. He says:

My grandfather, who worked at Raleigh bicycles, had been around at the very founding of the Labour Party in Nottingham. That was family folklore, anyway. It was certainly a fairly radical city and my grandfather was very involved in that. So we were talking about [politics] a lot [at home].

I wasted my time at school and deservedly left school without the qualifications I should have had. I started work in [a] warehouse. If you didn't reach a certain amount of production, you were fired. So as a kid who had just left school I had experience of seeing grown men being fired. That triggered my already strong belief in trade unions, and I got a trade union branch started at that warehouse which is still going strong today.

Faced with the hard grind of the working world, the teenage Graham Allen soon regretted his academic failure. 'I had to get up really early to get to work,' he says.

I had to get two buses; one bus took me into the city centre, and the other bus took me out the other side. And I do remember, one winter's morning, walking through the city centre square, which was called Slab Square, and the slush coming over my shoes and into my socks, and thinking: 'Just maybe, and I'd never admit it to them, my parents are right, I should have worked a bit harder at school'.

So he went back to the books, taking A-levels in his own

time, and winning a place at the Guildhall in London. 'What a difference a year can make,' he says.

> I was really turned on by learning about politics. I think because it didn't come easy in the first instance and I had to use a second chance, I was really taken by it and loved what I did there: politics, economics and sociology. I graduated first in my year.
>
> I'm not trying to claim I was a great academic, I was just really inspired and turned on by the opportunity to learn in a way probably I wouldn't have been if I had gone straight from school to university.

When his undergraduate degree ended, Mr Allen decided to do his Master's. He says:

> I could have gone to the LSE, but I chose to go to the University of Leeds, because Ralph Miliband [the socialist thinker and father of future senior Labour MPs David and Ed Miliband] was the professor there. I remember teaching cricket to the two young kids he'd got, David and Ed. I always say I never taught them anything about politics, but I taught them in the garden how to throw a really good outswinging cricket ball, which probably stood them in good stead for the rest of their lives. Ralph Miliband was fantastic – an electric, sparky sort of personality.

Following his MA, Mr Allen turned down a job offer to become a 'well-paid' trainee producer at the BBC in favour of taking up a position as 'a poorly paid researcher for the Labour Party'. 'It was much less money but more interesting to me,' he says. 'Long, long hours with the Labour Party, or the glamour of the BBC and being a producer, and I went with my heart.'

Mr Allen worked for Labour at its headquarters in London, first at Transport House then Woolworth Road, before moving on to become a bureaucrat at the Greater London Council (GLC). There he won praise for leading the opposition to a move by the Thatcher government to prevent trade unions funding the Labour Party.

He says:

It was just after the [1984–85] miners' strike. Everyone said: 'You're going to get hammered, trade unions are unpopular, trade unionists are unpopular.' It was an existential threat to the Labour Party. I had a free hand to run a national campaign with thirty-odd trade unions. At quite a young age, thirty-two or so, I was in the same room as, and having to be listened to by, all the senior trade union leaders. The campaign was incredibly successful. Not only did we win and maintain all the existing unions affiliated to the Labour Party, we ended up with six or five trade unions joining the Labour Party. So Mrs Thatcher had intended to reduce the Labour Party [but] it was actually the beginning, really, of the big fight back against Thatcherism. The tide turned at that point, so I was a minor celebrity. Which was helpful at that point when I went back home to seek the nomination for Nottingham North.

Flush from his success on the political funding campaign, Mr Allen was a shoo-in when a vacancy emerged in his home constituency of Nottingham North. In the general election held on 11 June 1987, he was elected with a majority of 1,665.

Arriving in the Commons the following week, he found Parliament familiar from his time with the Labour Party, but frustrating. 'I had been in and out of the House of Commons so it didn't overawe me,' he says. 'I went in thinking the place needed reform. It needed democracy, modernising.'

The campaign for greater democracy would be Mr Allen's driving force throughout his time in Parliament. As a first step, he teamed up with a group of fellow-thinking Labour MPs who wished to modernise the parliamentary party. 'It didn't keep minutes, didn't have a proper record of decisions, was very much led by the leadership in terms of keeping people in line,' he says.

Seeing the heavy drinking that used to go on at lunchtimes, I was [not impressed].

But that degree of radicalism which I started with, it was a trade-off; you either become one of the lads, become institutionalised, or you decided where you [stood] on certain things, and I made that decision fairly early on.

Without being disloyal, [I was dedicated to] trying to make the Labour Party more of a reformist and radical party than it was then, and remains today, sadly.

Despite feeling like he never became 'one of the lads', in his second term in the Commons, Mr Allen was invited to join the front bench, becoming a member of the shadow Social Security team. When Tony Blair became shadow Home Secretary, he moved to join him. Mr Allen says:

The job I enjoyed the most [in opposition] was working [for] Blair as the democratic reform person in the Home Affairs team. I did a lot of the formative stuff around the creation of the Supreme Court, what should happen on the second chamber, devolution, not only to the nations but the localities of the UK with [then Labour leader] John Smith. It was a great period, because John was a non-metropolitan person. Even though he was seen as a conventional politician, he didn't have that acquiescence that a lot of them have.

Following John Smith's early death and the election as

Labour leader of Tony Blair in 1994, Mr Allen bounced round several shadow teams, including Culture, Transport and the Environment. When the party emerged triumphant at the 1997 election, he became a government whip, a role which, in the light of Labour's overwhelming strength of numbers in the Commons, was far from challenging. There was never any doubt that the government would win its votes, meaning the whips were left with little to do.

Mr Allen says:

It was a landslide victory, [so] being in the Whips' Office was not very interesting to anyone with more than two brain cells. We had another big majority in 2001, and I asked Jonathan Powell [Mr Blair's Chief of Staff] to put me on the front bench or send me to the back benches, but I didn't want to be in the Whips' Office.

I was happy to serve, don't get me wrong, and was happy with the size of the victory in 1997, as we all were, but I'd done my shift. And Jonathan Powell said: 'You're known as being very independent-minded,' which is a sort of Sir Humphrey way of saying you're not just one of those people who will do what we tell you.

Content to return to the back benches, Mr Allen set about becoming, not quite a thorn in the side of the leadership, but certainly someone to be reckoned with, and whose support could not be taken for granted. He says:

I will always come up with, as I did in opposition, a trail of policy, whether it be the democratic agenda, or transport, or whatever brief I had. I may have rebelled once, I think, on foundation hospitals, but I was not a serial rebel. But, on the back benches I always traded my vote as expensively as I could. They knew I would always try and bargain, not just I'm going to vote against it come what may, which some of our colleagues would always do. If they could make a case then the prospect of me voting would improve.

Two years after leaving government, Mr Allen found himself helping to lead the greatest rebellion of the modern era, in opposition to Tony Blair's bid to go to war in Iraq. He says:

Iraq was a very cathartic moment. I was one of the organisers of the Iraq rebellion; the first e-rebellion in Parliament, the biggest rebellion [suffered by] a governing party in British political history. That always makes me feel a little bit ambivalent; I didn't want to vote against my party or my Prime Minister, but this was such a big issue, such an obviously disastrous decision to take.

I met Hans Blix [the UN weapons inspector]. There were no weapons of mass destruction. And why on earth [did] they choose Iraq? I think George Bush got Iraq and Iran mixed up. I haven't a clue how we ended up there. There were no Osama bin Laden supporters in Iraq because Saddam Hussein was as much a brutal dictator to them as anybody else.

I wasn't pacifistic, it just seemed to me totally outside the traditions of British foreign policy, and if you go into Iraq, what's to stop you going into twenty other dictatorships?

That probably in my bones was one of the points where I was deeply saddened I was unable to make an even bigger impact, actually. [My goal] is always to work cross-party, and I worked with Charles Kennedy [then Lib Dem leader], Ken Clarke [long-serving Conservative MP and former Cabinet minister], other people, to make sure we got as many people as possible [to oppose the war].

I worked on Labour MPs and we got forty-four in total. The majority of the free people in the Parliamentary Labour Party voted against the government [but] the payroll vote clinched it for the government.

Overall, I was proud of what I did, but sad that it came to that because, without hindsight, I wanted the Blair government to be a success but it was pretty obvious pretty quickly that this was what people would remember him for.

Could he have been more radical? Of course he could. But the fact was, he won elections and had been a good Prime Minister, and I'm afraid everyone will remember him for ever as the guy who took the lid off the religious wars in the Middle East. We are living with the consequences in Western Europe and elsewhere. I'm very sorry it went that way, but it was a defining moment in Labour Party history.

On a personal level, Mr Allen's opposition to the war had a direct impact on his career. 'I was immediately off Tony Blair's Christmas card list, obviously, and any chance of getting back on the slippery slope and of being recognised on merit, doing a ministerial job, that went out of the window big time at that point,' he says.

Recognising his limited clout on the national stage, Mr Allen was thrilled when soon afterwards he was asked by the City of Nottingham to chair their local strategic partnership [LSP], a coming together of services including the police and healthcare to target regeneration. He was the first MP to chair an LSP, and used his time to make Nottingham the first 'early intervention city' in the country. The plan involved targeting resources at youngsters at the earliest possible stage in life, before they could become a major problem and corresponding drain on the state.

He says:

My constituency is one of the most deprived in the UK. It is a tough area of white working-class former council estates. It seemed to me that we were attacking symptoms all the time, trying to get kids at sixteen to up their grades rather than saying, 'How on earth did this start? Why did this kid not get A-levels? This kid's got a brain.' I got very interested in all this stuff about how you do better at primary school. The primaries say kids arrive at four or five unable to speak in sentences, unable to recognise numbers and letters. How do we help before that point? How do we help parents? How do we give every kid social and emotional capability? You have to start before the child is born by helping the potential parents-to-be before they are thinking about sex. You have got a virtuous circle. If you go back round that cycle you can actually start to impact on things that are going to happen eighteen years later, so those kids do go to university. So Nottingham pioneered early intervention projects.

In his work on early intervention, Mr Allen has teamed up with some unlikely partners on a cross-party basis, including Iain Duncan Smith, the right-of-centre former Conservative leader and Work and Pensions Secretary. 'We were a very odd coupling,' Mr Allen says. 'I don't agree with Iain on anything else; can't get a cigarette paper between us on early intervention. We wrote a book together.'

Following the 2010 election, the new Conservative Prime Minister, David Cameron, asked Mr Allen to produce an independent report on early intervention. He was pleased with the result, which led to the establishment of the Early Intervention Foundation.

Another high from Mr Allen's later years in Parliament was his chairmanship of the Constitutional Reform Oversight Committee, which produced a draft written constitution.

Today, he remains despondent about what he describes as 'a political system which is not fit for purpose'. He is also unimpressed with the current relationship between politics and the media. 'Parliament is so weak,' he says.

Something I had realised all along that I'd hoped I could do something about was to have the Labour Party in power thinking more long-term [with] less day-to-day responsiveness. You've got to do more than what might placate the newspapers in the short term. There is the embryo [now] of the House of Commons being able to do a more effective job, but it has to separate itself from the executive, and I don't think we're anywhere near that at the moment.

Mr Allen believes the current swing to the left which has taken place in the Labour Party under Jeremy Corbyn is a direct result of what he sees as the lost opportunities of the Blair era. 'The Labour Party has lost its way a little bit,' he says. 'People talk about Jeremy Corbyn; Jeremy Corbyn didn't create Jeremy Corbyn. There is a longer basis to this. We all need to look to ourselves in terms of what we did to enable that to happen.'

Mr Allen sees the governments of Tony Blair as a lost opportunity. He says:

There seem to have been a number of big chances missed. The Labour government did a lot of good stuff, but, you know what, I'm greedy. I expect a Labour government to do good stuff on education and health. I expect that basic stuff to be done, and it was, and I'm thankful for it. I think Labour should also have a longer-term perspective about social change, about political development, about education in its deepest sense, about what it means to be a member of our community and how to build a future for children. Because we didn't have the ideological drive, Tony Blair's government and MPs including himself compromised too much to win elections, because they lacked a long-term perspective about what they wanted to achieve.

Tony Blair was actually what he appeared to be, which was a decent, middle-class person, with little ideological drive. There wasn't, behind that, someone who said that 'I think transforming our society and the opportunities for working-class people in this country is what keeps me awake at night.'

Were it not for his ill-health, Mr Allen would have happily stayed on in Parliament for another term. He says:

> [It] means my soft tissue around my joints gets eroded. They didn't find this early enough to stop it. It's stopped now, but the damage is done, unfortunately. So I've had a new hip, and a new knee, and this February I had a new ankle, so I'm just now walking again. I've got to have the left done now, probably in October.

When Theresa May called the early election for June 2017, Mr Allen came close to opting to remain, but, given his medical issues, became concerned that he would not be able to give his 'formidable' caseload the attention it deserved. 'I was desperately anxious that if I didn't go again then someone would [have to] look after my constituency,' he says. 'I need[ed] somebody who was going to be 100 per cent, seven days a week. The hard work often starts when you get home to Nottingham on a Thursday or Friday morning. And then back again to London Sunday night.' Mr Allen was 'relieved' with the selection of his successor, Alex Norris, and campaigned for him during the election.

He intends to keep on campaigning on the issues he holds dear outside of Parliament, particularly early intervention and his work on democratic reform. 'I will continue to press for those without being a prisoner in the open prison of the House of Commons,' he says.

I'm a political entrepreneur and I think I can do that outside of the House of Commons. Looking at what I have done, very little of it needed the physical platform of the House of Commons. In terms of hanging round the House of Commons for pointless votes at 10.30 on a Monday night, actually I've never seen that achieve anything for anybody, never mind me.

I've been incredibly lucky. I get a salary slip every month and I don't look at them. Anybody that does a job they love, as strenuous, challenging, as frustrating as it is, and gets paid for it as well, that happens to very few people, without being trite about it.

I still haven't won everyone over, so I better keep going. Hopefully we'll get there in my lifetime – or my daughter's lifetime.

CV

Born and raised in Nottingham, researcher for the Labour Party, campaigner on the Greater London Council.

1987   elected MP for Nottingham North.
1991   becomes shadow Social Security minister.

1992   becomes shadow Home Affairs minister.

1994   becomes shadow Culture minister.

1995   becomes shadow Transport minister.

1996   becomes shadow Environment minister.

1997   becomes government whip.

2001   returns to back benches.

2003   helps lead opposition to war in Iraq.

2010   becomes chairman of the Political and Constitutional Reform Committee.

Married to Allyson, one daughter.

PAT GLASS

Pat Glass, 60, was Labour MP for North West Durham 2010–17.

How did you end up in Parliament?

'It was never an intention. But I live in the North East, and the MP at the time was standing down, and it was a woman-only shortlist. There wasn't a single woman from the constituency standing, so there was a huge amount of pressure put on by my local branch.'

How did you feel on first becoming an MP?

'There were lots of people that I knew within the party already, so it wasn't in that sense an alien place. What I found alien about it was the culture that exists in there, in particular, I have to say, on the Tory benches. I hadn't come across that level of sexism since 1973.'

Best of times:
'One of the high points for me was the building of a new school in the constituency. I knew from my days in the civil service [that] to be a good constituency MP you have pretty much got to be a good stalker and I stalked [Education Secretary] Michael Gove.'

Worst of times:
'I had an absolutely awful time during the [EU] referendum. I became a target of the Vote Leave trolling, and it was really horrible. That, ultimately, was the reason I decided I'm not going to do this any more.'

Why are you leaving?
'I am nearly sixty-one. There are people who go on forever, but I don't necessarily think that's a good idea. I think there is room for new people there, and people can stay too long, so I decided to go after two terms. Now, when the election was called [early], I had to make a decision. It's not the kind of job you can say, "Well, I'll do two years and then I'll go." You have got to make a commitment for five years. And I just thought, I can't make a commitment for five years. That would make me sixty-six, sixty-seven,

and I just don't want to do that. It's a hard job. It's hard on all your family. I have had big jobs for a long time and I just want a chance to sit down, let somebody else do it.'

What are your thoughts for future MPs?
'They have to be good to themselves and their families, because this is a really heavy job. It is all-consuming, and you have to carve out time for your family in particular because otherwise they suffer. It just takes over. And I have seen it, I have seen so many MPs, politics is all they do. They don't have anything else other than that. And that's rather sad. For many of them this will be new. London is a city they don't necessarily know very well, so my advice would be to give themselves time and above everything else be kind to themselves and their family.'

Will you have any regrets about leaving the Commons? And what are you going to do next?
'I have never been one of those people who cry over spilt milk. I remember my grandma used to say: "Turn to the plough and never look back." I have always been like that, whatever role I have been in.

I am quite keen on maybe doing some voluntary work. I have got lots of skills from Parliament but also before, and those kind of things are particularly useful now education is so splintered and fractured and in many areas a real mess. So we will see what comes along. If nothing comes along I am absolutely fine.'

PAT GLASS: THE FULL STORY

Pat Glass had never planned to become an MP, and it's fair to say she did not come to love the House of Commons in the way most Members do. Nor is she particularly sad to be leaving after seven years in Parliament. Born in County Durham, she says:

> I was from a political family but I was never the one who was intended to be an MP. My father was a trade union officer, so we talked politics at breakfast, but I went into education, I had a whole career in education, at school, local and national level. I was director of education [in Sunderland and Greenwich], and just before going into Parliament I was a senior government adviser at the DfE [Department for Education].

Given her background, there was never any question that Mrs Glass would be a Labour supporter. But while she was a member of her local party, she says her role in local government meant she was never particularly active before becoming an MP.

The Labour Party respects the kinds of principles that I think are important, things like fairness, things that are important to me, important to my family, and, yes, it was always Labour, it was never anything else. A lot of the time I was politically restricted so the extent of my involvement could be very limited. I went to the local branch meeting and I delivered leaflets at election time and that was my entire involvement.

In the run-up to the 2010 general election, the long-standing MP in North West Durham, the former Labour Cabinet minister Hilary Armstrong, stood down. The mood in the local party was for someone from the constituency to replace her. But when an all-women shortlist was imposed on the selection, and no local female candidates emerged, Mrs Glass found herself coming under pressure to throw her hat into the ring. She had mixed feelings – and continues to do so.

People knew what I did and therefore they knew that I was a woman who was capable of handling big jobs, big decisions, but also I think they knew where I came from. I had to think about it a great deal, because it was a significant cut in salary. I know MPs get paid OK, and you don't like to mention that, but that was one of the reasons [I was equivocal]. And also because I was going from one of the most well thought of professions to one of the least well thought of professions. So that was a lot to think about, but in the end I decided I would. I went for selection and was selected very late, the end of February, and the election was in May 2010.

With Mrs Armstrong having held the seat with double digit majorities for her entire time in Parliament, Mrs Glass could be confident on becoming the Labour candidate that she would go on to be elected as the area's MP. She says:

Anything can happen in an election, but, to be fair, getting selected was the issue in a seat like mine. It's a solid, safe Labour seat, so if you were selected, unless there was an absolute disaster, then you were going to be elected. So although I had candidate-itis – I was convinced I was going to be the first Labour candidate [in] forever to lose North West Durham – that isn't what happened.

Election night passed in a blur. 'It was a complete daze,' Mrs Glass says.

I remember the Returning Officer handing me an envelope and saying: 'Those are your joining instructions.' It was four o'clock in the morning; it just became a real daze. I went home, went to bed, and my husband took me away to Lindisfarne [Holy Island, off the Northumberland coast] for a couple of days, just to kind of get our heads back together before I was due to go to Parliament on the Tuesday.

Arriving in the Commons, Mrs Glass found herself in familiar, yet at times uncomfortably hostile, territory.

I had been in there lots of times in my role working for the DfE, because I had worked closely with Ed Balls, so I had been in [Parliament before]. And I also knew lots of people. Ian Mearns, who is the MP for Gateshead, and [I] went in together. I have known Ian since I was sixteen.

It's a very difficult place, particularly I think as a young woman. I had had a career, I had been used to being, for many years, the only woman in situations. For years I was the only woman on the Secondary Heads Group, so I was used to that kind of thing. But for a young woman, I think it can be quite an alien place. When you get up and speak in the Commons, the camera is on you, it isn't on the people opposite. They can make gestures, shout, and that's what they do, and some of them are not very nice. Now [the Conservatives] have got more women on their side and that seems to have calmed it down, since 2015, but they are still not very pleasant. And they are worse with the young women.

Mrs Glass struggled to settle into her new life in the Commons, and found the MPs' lifestyle an unhealthy one, suited only to political obsessives. 'I enjoyed the constituency stuff; I enjoyed the stuff in Parliament [less],' she says.

It was a job. I went there and I did it; I'm glad I don't have to do it any more. I did think it was a fantastic place and I was incredibly privileged and lucky to be there, but it does have its downsides. It's a lonely life. Although I have lots of friends, and all the time I was there I shared a flat so I always had a friend to go home to, I think for a lot of people it can be quite lonely. Because I was older, because I had had a career, because I wasn't terribly interested in climbing the greasy pole or anything like that, I think it was easier for me, whereas for other people it's hard to make friends.

I remember one politician coming to my [constituency] house. We were doing something in the village where I live, and afterwards we came back to have something to eat, and stayed the night. I have got a nice house, I had it before I was an MP – I couldn't afford it now. She was talking to somebody and said: 'She has got this lovely house and this wonderful garden, she's even got a dog.'

And I thought it sounded so sad. [Many MPs] don't have those. They just do politics.

While Mrs Glass was used to the pressures of what she describes as 'big jobs,' she fears for new MPs arriving in the Commons who may not appreciate the strain parliamentary life is likely place on them and their families. She says:

For me, I had worked in London for years before becoming an MP, going down on a Monday and coming back on a Friday. Previously, [when I w]as Director of Education, it wasn't a nine to five [job] and [it] took all of your time and you [had] to give 100 per cent to it. I did, I look back now and think, to the detriment, not massively, but of my family. I never went to a parents' evening; my husband did. I was always out in the morning first and back last at night. So for [my family] me being an MP was just a little bit extra.

Unlike most MPs, Mrs Glass was not ambitious for ministerial office, and the promotions which came her way were a mixed blessing. She says:

Almost from the beginning, because of my background, I was on the front bench, but I really wasn't striving for it. I didn't want to be Prime Minister; I didn't want to be

Leader of the Opposition. I never got the opportunity to be a backbencher, and I think that that meant that some of the parts of the House of Commons were kind of closed to me. People get involved in things like the Commonwealth, they go on trips abroad – I never really did any of that. I was on the front bench, and it's onerous on the front bench. When you are there you have got to be absolutely up to speed with everything.

Despite her feeling of having missed out on life as a backbencher, Mrs Glass found that her first role in opposition, as a shadow Education minister, brought some satisfaction. 'I quite enjoyed being on the front bench,' she says.

It's not as nerve-racking as people think. The first time I ever stood up in Parliament, I sat down [again] and my knees were like jelly, it was about six months in. But, actually, standing at the despatch box [as a frontbench spokesman], you have something to hold on to and you have control of the conversation. So I enjoyed that. Obviously at the time it all feels rather stressful.

As far as she could with the demands of her frontbench duties, Mrs Glass focused on her constituency. She says:

I wanted to be a really good constituency MP. You opened

an envelope in my constituency and I was there. I tried very hard to raise the profile of the MP in the constituency. I enjoyed the constituency side very much. I'm hoping that I have made a really hard job for the girl who is going to take over from me, Laura [Pidcock], to live up to.

Characteristically, Mrs Glass's high point in her time as an MP came when she secured funds for a new school in her area, which had originally been planned under the Labour government's Building Schools for the Future programme and then scrapped by the coalition government. Mrs Glass launched a one-woman campaign targeting Michael Gove, the Education Secretary. 'I literally stalked that man,' she says.

In fact, when he rang me to tell me that the government had come up with £20 million, he said: 'Where are you?' Because I was on my mobile. And I said, 'I am actually in Brittany,' and he said, 'I thought [so], because you haven't rung me this week.' Having previously been in the civil service I knew that ministers are not professional. I had been a director of education; I knew the way the system worked. Ministers are not like that. They just want people off their case. I knew that because I had seen it. And I knew that the way to get something was to really harass them.

At the start of 2016, Mrs Glass was promoted to the role of shadow Europe minister, a key role with the referendum on Britain's membership of the European Union six months away. But it was not a happy time for the Labour Party. Mrs Glass was now serving as No. 2 to Hilary Benn, the shadow Foreign Secretary, a man she would come to respect and admire. However, the relationship between Mr Benn and figures in the leadership around Jeremy Corbyn had come under strain due to disagreements over policy on bombing Syria, and the problems would intensify as the referendum grew closer. Moderates in the parliamentary party accused Mr Corbyn, who had historically been a Eurosceptic, of failing to campaign with any enthusiasm for the Remain cause. Mrs Glass says:

One of the most wonderful people I worked with in Parliament was Hilary Benn. But that was like walking on a tightrope with the leader's office. There were lots of tensions there between the shadow Foreign Office staff and the leader's office, and I was kind of going back and forth between the two. And then Hilary was sacked. That was not a pleasant time, actually a really awful time, because I worked really well with Hilary and we became quite good friends.

Jeremy Corbyn's decision to dismiss Mr Benn came amid

rising anger among moderates about the lacklustre referendum campaign, and corresponding suspicion of them in the leadership. Within days, the row would escalate into a full-blown coup, with mass resignations from the shadow Cabinet and other frontbench positions. Mrs Glass found herself at the centre of events. She says:

On the Saturday afternoon [following the referendum], I got a phone call from Jeremy Corbyn offering me the shadow Secretary of State job for Education. And with my background [in education], that was kind of amazing. So I said yes to that, texted Hilary and said [I had been given shadow] Secretary of State for Education, he said, congratulations, and then he rang me the next day to say Jeremy had sacked him. That was awful. Then the next morning, Monday, Tuesday, the world fell apart and everybody resigned. And in the end I kind of thought, however much I love this job, I cannot stay in this situation at this time. So I resigned as well. So I was shadow Secretary of State for Education for a very short time. I did enjoy it when I was first offered the job. But there we are. You have to be at the centre of the storm to see what these things are like.

As she announced her resignation from the shadow Cabinet after just three days, Mrs Glass came to another big decision: she would not remain an MP after the next election. In her resignation statement, she explained that her high-profile role speaking for Labour on the issue of Europe during the referendum campaign had led to her becoming the target of 'Vote Leave trolls'. She was subjected to vicious abuse, including death threats, and began to look forward to quitting the Commons in 2020 when, under the Fixed Term Parliament Act, the next general election was due to be held.

When the coup against Mr Corbyn failed, and he won re-election in September 2016, Mrs Glass agreed to rejoin his team. She says:

> I was only a backbencher for a very short period again because things started to pick up again. I was asked, would you come back, and what would you like to do? I thought, I'm quite interested in rail, it's [an area] where we have a policy and it's publicly supported. So I went back as shadow Rail minister and did that until the election.

When the general election turned out to be three years earlier than Mrs Glass anticipated, she knew it was an option for her to stand again. She was not tempted. And, having quit the Commons, she is in no doubt now that it was the right time for her to leave. 'I have never worried about looking back over things,' she says.

I have made the decision, and I think it is the right decision. It has coincided almost to the day with my mother being really ill, and I'm not sure how, as a family, we would have managed if I hadn't been here. So it was the right time for me and for them and so I don't regret it at all. Honestly, I have got lots of other things going on in my life. I have grandchildren that I never see.

Since announcing that she would indeed be departing the Commons at the general election, Mrs Glass has felt both a sense of relief and, in the end, a sense of pride at what she has achieved, in the constituency if not in Parliament.

Certainly I have had lots of people contacting me, even [some] people saying, I am a member of the Conservative Party but you are the best MP we have ever had. That was really nice to get.

The girl who is taking over as the Labour candidate is quite young, she is twenty-nine. She's really excited, she is a real activist, she is working hard, and I think she will do a good job. I have said to her, 'Look, I will give you all the advice that you ask for, and I will be there if you want me to be there, but other than that I won't.' And I think that that is something I will stick to, because I have seen too many ex-MPs is interfering with their successors, and I just think it's hers now. She will make a good MP. I will give her whatever advice she wants, but if she doesn't want it then that's absolutely fine with me. [On election night] I think I'll feel all those things I used to feel before I was an MP; worried, anxious, but I won't want to be there. It's somebody else's time.

Following her retirement from the Commons, Mrs Glass is in no hurry to find another 'big job'. She says:

I have had a number of approaches, and what I have said to people is I don't want to do anything in London, nothing full-time, and nothing until after the summer. I am intending to spend February in Spain when we get the bad weather. We are doing all of those kinds of things that people who live normal lives do.

CV

Born and raised in Co. Durham, worked for local education authorities and as a civil servant at the Department for Education.

2010   elected MP for North West Durham.

2015   becomes shadow Education minister.

2016   becomes shadow Europe minister; becomes shadow
Education Secretary; resigns from front bench;
announces she is standing down; becomes shadow
Rail minister.

2017   stands down from Parliament.

Married to Bob, three children.